Why Men Have
AFFAIRS

~ Understanding the
Hidden Motives of Infidelity ~

REAL LIFE SOLUTIONS FOR
MEN, WOMEN AND COUPLES

Irwin M. Marcus, M.D.

Notice:
This book is intended as a reference guide, not as a medical manual.
The information given here is designed to help you make informed
decisions about your health. It is not intended as a substitute for any
treatment that may have been prescribed to you by your doctor or
therapist. If you suspect that you have a medical or emotional
problem, we urge you to seek competent medical or psychiatric help.

Submit all requests for reprinting to:
Greenleaf Book Group LLC
4425 Mo Pac South, Suite 600
Longhorn Bldg., 3rd Floor
Austin, TX 78735
(512) 891-6100

Published in the United States by
Bon Temps Press
New Orleans, LA

Cover Design and Layout by Francine Smith

Second Edition

Other books by Irwin M. Marcus, M.D.

The Family Book of Childcare
with Niles Newton, Ph.D., Paul Gyorgy, M.D.
and Thaddeus L. Montgomery, M.D.

Currents in Psychoanalysis

Masturbation: From Infancy to Senescence
with John J. Francis, M.D.

ACKNOWLEDGMENTS

I hope this book will honor the courageous men who trusted me with the rich material and taught me what their affairs were really about. It wasn't about sex.

Second, to my wife, Angela, who gave me her loving encouragement and emotional support. She even laughs at my silly jokes. To my deceased wife, Dorothy, who taught me about the magic of a good marriage. My appreciation also goes out to my three children-Randall, Sherry and Melinda. My thanks to Robin Quinn for transcribing my handwritten manuscript and for her editorial suggestions.

I am very appreciative of Bon Temps Press and Fred Snyder, the publisher and editor-in-chief. Finally, I want to thank Meredith Bernstein and her Literary Agency in New York for her encouragement and efforts along the road.

Why Men Have

AFFAIRS

~ Understanding the
Hidden Motives of Infidelity ~

REAL LIFE SOLUTIONS FOR
MEN, WOMEN AND COUPLES

Irwin M. Marcus, M.D.

CONTENTS

1   Introduction / **1**

2   Stuck in Adolescence: The Adulteen / **9**

3   Just Having Fun: The Playmate / **29**

4   Simply for the Thrill: The Pleasure Seeker / **46**

5   High on Conquest: The Conquistador / **60**

6   Seeking Variety: The Sampler / **73**

7   A Need for Independence: The Yankee Doodle / **88**

8   Addicted to Excitement: The Daredevil / **102**

9   Anxiety About Aging: The Ponce de Léon / **115**

10   Searching for a New Spouse: The Groom / **128**

11   Struggling with More Severe Problems Troubled Men / **140**

12   Summary / **159**

      Closing Thoughts / **170**

      A Note About Aids / **173**

      Suggested Reading / **175**

CHAPTER ONE

Introduction

A life without love,
without the presence of the beloved,
is nothing but a mere magic-lantern show.
We draw out slide after slide,
swiftly tiring of each,
and pushing it back
to make haste for the next.

– ELECTIVE AFFINITIES, BY JOHANN WOLFGANG VON GOETHE, GERMAN POET,
DRAMATIST, NOVELIST AND SCIENTIST (1749-1832)

On a crisp sunny Sunday afternoon in fall, a season when New Orleans treats us to nice breezy weather, I was comfortably seated on the porch and was in the middle of a lively conversation on whatever you talk about at a cocktail party. From another area, Richard came strolling over unnoticed and suddenly whispered into my ear, "Do you really want to know why men have affairs?" I was startled, being jerked from the subject under discussion. Still I managed to smile and replied, "OK, Richard, what's the real reason?" He leaned toward my ear and whispered, "Sex." Then Richard turned and smugly walked away, appearing to be very satisfied with his insightful self.

I had just met Richard earlier that day at the party. However, over the years, several of my male friends had volunteered similar words of wisdom when they learned about the subject of this book, *Why Men Have Affairs*. My response is that the book is about the very guys who think they know why men have affairs yet don't really understand the reasons!

Our society's grasp of the "why" of infidelity varies widely and much has been written about it. Why should I add to this robust literature? Drawing on what I have gleaned from my forty years of experience in treating men who have affairs, I don't agree with many of the current explanations.

I don't agree, for example, that it's a man's biological makeup or his hormones that cause him to be unfaithful. I don't agree, for example, that infidelity is due to the increased number of available partners as more women are involved in the workplace. I don't agree, for example, that a man's gender creates the unzipping reflex.

Men may not be able to control their fantasies but they can control their actions. For those who feel that "Men will be men," I must point out that this statement dismisses judgment. I believe that affairs are not the result of "maleness," but, rather, a deliberate, conscious decision influenced by the troubles and weaknesses which are within them. Men can be monogamous!

Looking Deeper for Answers

At the time of their affairs, most men don't recognize that there is a risk to their married life. These men all believed that they were too smart to get caught. My patients were all intelligent men who wouldn't take big risks for small gains. The gains they experienced from the affairs were very important to them at the time. Only later, looking back in retrospect, did these men decide that the affairs weren't worth it.

What Is an Affair?

There is a multitude of opinions on what constitutes an affair. *Why Men Have Affairs* focuses on heterosexual marriages, thus I consider an affair to be an extramarital sexual relationship with a partner other than a spouse. Using this framework, the so-called "one-night stand" would not be an affair because it is a brief sexual encounter without a continuing association; no relationship exists. One night stands are forms of cheating and cheating is a much more broad category. However, if a wife finds out about a husband's one-night stand, she is still likely to feel hurt and this discovery can also be damaging to a marriage.

A fantasy affair would not be an affair because it's entirely mental rather than part of the real world and there is no relationship involved. Also, an ongoing close relationship between a man and a woman without any physical sex does not meet my definition of an affair, either. Still, even within this framework, not all affairs are alike. Some are oriented much more toward sex while others contain much more interest in a relationship. The differing makeup of affairs can be illustrated as seen in this diagram.

Categories of Affairs

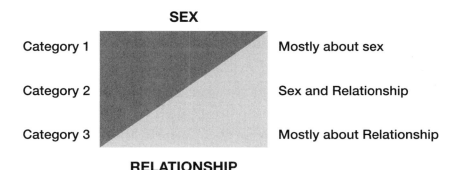

SEX

Category 1	Mostly about sex
Category 2	Sex and Relationship
Category 3	Mostly about Relationship

RELATIONSHIP

Over time, as bonding begins, a couple may evolve from one category of affair to another. Thus, an affair starting in Category One, where the emphasis is on sex, could end up as a Category Three where the focus is on the relationship. The reverse transition is also possible. Can a person "fall in love" during an affair in any of these categories? Yes, because falling in love is so full of fantasy that one can manufacture love even when the affair is mostly sexual activity.

What is sex?

According to an American Medical Association Journal article based on a survey of young males, many men don't view oral sex as "sex." Yet other adults would disagree and may view oral sex as an even more intimate form of sexual activity than intercourse.

For our purposes, I will define sexual activity as an orgasm induced by any means whatsoever through any interaction with another person. Even more broadly, I'd say that if one partner is arousing another, whether that attention is returned or not, the relationship is partly sexual.

Some Words on My Study & Approach

The data on infidelity upon which this book is based was gathered over four decades and involved a wide range of men who came to me for therapy. They were men in their twenties and on into their seventies. The duration of their marriages varied from several months to over fifty years. These men came from diverse backgrounds and had a variety of occupations. Although they were primarily college-educated men, almost all had earned high school diplomas. While a few of the men did come for a consultation and/or therapy because of the affairs they were having, most sought therapy for other reasons: occupational issues, personal problems or marital difficulties. Therapy for the affairs they were having followed the discovery of the source of their problems. In the course of our work together, these men revealed information about their affairs. Over time, the deeper motivations for the infidelity became clear. As the men were treated from anywhere to a few months to several years, the study was both intensive and extensive.

Consistently the majority of men in therapy did not want to end their marriages although they were well aware that they were breaking their marital commitment. Therefore, for the women who are engaged in an affair, heed this warning. If you are one of those women who are having affairs with married men in the hopes that your lovers will eventually leave their wives and offer a permanent committed relationship, I must say that the odds are against it. While the odds might not be as high as trying to win a state lottery, there's still only a slight chance it will happen. Furthermore, if he does divorce his wife and marry you, then he'll probably be unfaithful with you as well. Some profiles of men having affairs include strings of marriages.

On a positive note for wives who are struggling with infidelity in their marriages, with treatment, most of these men stopped having affairs and turned back to their wives and families. Once the men in therapy saw through their pat answers and began to understand the real motivations for their affairs, they started to look at themselves and marriage with a different perspective. When the destructive patterns in their behavior were recognized, the driven and compulsive nature of their behavior changed. Most of the men having affairs heal when they find better methods for coping with their anxiety and depression.

If men have affairs because of their own inner problems, then looking at past experiences must be emphasized in recovery. Currently, in modern therapy, there's a strong current flowing away from history and toward giving people a quick fix. This approach ignores the influence of the past in all of our actions. A quick fix is great if it is held into the future but many times it cannot be held because many people cannot do what they, themselves, know should be done until they thoroughly understand why they are doing what they do. They simply have too little knowledge about the true motivations for their present actions to make a permanent change. People walking on a path to the future are on a road made from their history. We are all currently living our history. If we don't understand the influence of our pasts, then we're going to find our present lives confusing. Understanding our histories gives us continuity. Whether we learn from self-help, social interactions, marriage or a therapist, real growth takes time because it involves coming to terms with the past.

Simply telling a man to stop having affairs does not change the man's attitude or his marital relationship. But, by understanding his past, a man is able to see why he's driving down familiar roads that lead nowhere. This understanding becomes an effective tool to use in building a new map which he can then use to move in new and healthier directions.

What's Ahead?

In the following chapters, you will meet ten very special groups of men. While each group has a different type of history featuring different threads and themes, they all represent profiles with a similar bundle of influences in their histories. You'll meet the Adulteen, the Playmate, the Pleasure Seeker, the Conquistador, the Sampler, the Daredevil and others. As these profiles suggest, men who have affairs suffer from weaknesses at their core and those weaknesses drive both the affairs and the types of affairs these men seek.

Men do want to understand more about what motivates an affair. I've listened to them in my office and at social gatherings for decades. This book is written to help them.

This book is also for wives and for women involved in affairs.

If wives understand why their husbands are having affairs, then several things happen. First, wives realize that the affair is not caused by them, that the affair is not their fault and that the affair is a symptom of a deep despair within their husbands. Next, wives learn how they can help their husbands during the healing process. Then, and most importantly, wives will experience a deeper intimacy with their husbands as the experience of working together to achieve a mutual goal bears fruit. Infidelity can be treated and, thereby, removed from the problems even healthy marriages encounter.

For the mistresses of these men, the motivations for the affairs are revealed and the prospects for a more permanent relationship are provided. The "other woman" can find herself here once she finds which profile fits her lover. She will know how long the affair will last, she will know what he really thinks of her and she will know exactly what her prospects for a more intimate relationship are.

Affairs do not have to lead to divorce unless other factors are present and unyielding. Surprisingly, many marriages actually grow to an even more satisfying level than that which existed before the infidelity took place as the couple learns to work together to solve a problem. A crisis can produce the energy needed for making changes.

If a marriage threatened by an affair is to be saved, then both people must be motivated to make it happen. Each spouse needs to see the affair as a challenge and a call to do the work needed to salvage the relationship. At the end of every chapter, comments on how this can be accomplished are included and insights which make recovery easier are offered.

A Final Note

I appreciate the trust my patients have placed in me. I deeply admire and respect their efforts to become better people as I know the courage it takes to face fear and accept change.

Therefore, I have not revealed their true identities. The men introduced in the next ten chapters are composites of hundreds of patients who have told me their stories. Any similarity to anyone, living or dead, is a coincidence as no single case example represents a single individual.

Now, let's meet the Adulteen.

CHAPTER TWO

Stuck in Adolescence: The Adulteen

Don't laugh at a youth
for his affections:
he is only trying on one face
after another
to find a face of his own.

– AFTERTHOUGHTS, BY LOGAN PEARSALL SMITH,
AMERICAN ESSAYIST & CRITIC (1865-1946)

Fifty-nine-year-old Anthony, a V.P. at a major oil company, could not sit still during our first session. Filled with fear, this former high-school football quarterback was pacing the floor. "I've been having sex with Irene for the past year and now she wants me to leave my wife. She's been threatening to call Julia and tell her that I want a divorce. She's so ungrateful. Don't I pay for all the expensive gifts and the living arrangements? I don't want a divorce." Anthony stopped for a moment and looked me straight in the eye. "I've been married to Julia for over 20 years and she's still beautiful and dresses great. We have three teenaged children. I love my wife and kids."

Anthony started pacing again. "Irene tells me she loves me and wants us to get married. She says I should see a therapist 'cause I tell her I love her, too, but I don't have the courage to divorce Julia. I think Irene's the problem. I don't have problems, except for the threats."

Anthony sighed and plopped down into an armchair. Looking toward the ceiling, he admitted, "You see, I've had a lot of women both before and during my marriage. Before Irene they would only scream and cry when I dropped them. It isn't until I get tired of them that they start cursing me and telling me what a self-centered bastard I am. Some have been quiet and shocked while others have threatened suicide. An affair is an affair and they knew I was married. Why make a federal case of it? They're getting something out of it and I never promised marriage. Of course, I tell them that I'm not happy with my wife but they like to hear that. It's a line all men use."

During our subsequent therapy sessions, Anthony revealed himself as a powerhouse with explosive tendencies at work, intimidating everyone in his department. He wasn't the kind of guy other men would challenge. Anthony felt superior to everyone, including his own boss, and he was insensitive to the feelings of other people. Although he would listen to my comments without long-lasting resentment, Anthony usually held a permanent grudge against anyone who criticized him. Seeing himself as being always right, he was prepared to out-shout and out-argue those who risked disagreeing with him.

Despite his flaws, Anthony was courageous and responsible in many ways. His bravery and conscientiousness were evident in his determination to seek help despite his heavy schedule. I grew to like and respect Anthony and was happy when we could talk to each other without having another shouting match.

"I came here feeling that my wife wasn't enough of a woman for me and discovered that I wasn't yet a man," Anthony acknowledged. "It was a bitter pill to swallow. Many times I left your office angry."

The Adulteen Personality

Optimally, we experience growth in our personality throughout our lives but the paths are different for different people. While some of us move successfully from adolescence to adulthood, others remain emotionally stuck in an earlier stage of life. These individuals go from graduation to work, to marriage and parenthood, perhaps even to the empty nest and retirement, while still continuing to see the world as they did during their teen years.

The Adulteen's failed transition from his adolescence into a more mature adult perspective often results in two predominate behaviors: uninhibited sexual activity and blatant aggression. Breaking the marriage commitment by having an affair is part of the Adulteen's sexual pattern. As if he were still a teenager, the Adulteen views sex as a forbidden act and this attitude increases and intensifies his pleasure. Some Adulteens think of sex as dirty, reinforcing this view with the use of obscene language while having sex.

Because they are aggressive, the Adulteen can be very successful and quite competitive in his career even when the Adulteen's raw competitiveness is combined with the insensitivity of an adolescent. Stepping on others and crushing anyone in their path, especially in business, is not unusual for these men. In their world, competitiveness, domination and control validates the masculinity of the Adulteen. They will be aggressive at work, in sports, in their marriages and in pursuing multiple sex partners. Adulteens tend to take on the world on their own terms because their self-centeredness is inflated while their interest in others is diminished.

Consequently, Adulteens have serious problems with intimacy. Hidden feelings of vulnerability and inadequacy become integrated into their personality during adolescence. These suppressed feelings prompt Adulteens to put up defensive facades. The central issue underneath their limited ability to accept intimacy lies in their fear of exposing their concealed emotional needs, their weak self-concept, their dependency, insecurity about their masculinity and their distrust of others.

A common element evident in the Adulteen profile is a lack of healthy role models for relationships within the original family. Since children and adolescents replicate the patterns of behavior they see at home, parents who are distant and superficial in both their marriage and parenting style set the tone for communicating and relating within the family. The children, having been born into this world, accept this pattern as being normal. Despite his immature perspectives, an Adulteen can, under favorable circumstances, mature and, much like a butterfly does, emerge from his teenage cocoon of problems into a mature, healthy and stable adult.

How the Adulteen Relates to His Mistress

The Adulteen wants his mistress to admire him, not to challenge him. He seeks total submission and total loyalty from her. While he doesn't care if she "has a brain" or not, she must be good-looking. He will dominate her to assure himself of his attractiveness, masculinity and his importance in the high school of life. If the Adulteen wants to cheat on his lover, he does. However, if she strays on him, then he will turn on her, with or without physical abuse, and usually end the relationship.

Driven by his desire for pleasure, the Adulteen has a low tolerance for frustration everywhere in his life including in his affairs. He rarely postpones gratification. The Adulteen's affairs tend to be short-lived, being a Category One or a weak Category Two. However, even in a Category Two affair, his attachment to his mistress is shallow. An Adulteen can detach himself from the affair without even looking back.

Often deceptive and cunning in the way he approaches a potential mistress, the Adulteen may ask the woman to lunch and act very formal during the meal while he assesses his chances. He might even ask another man to join them to create an appearance of innocence. Once he thinks his foot is in the door, the Adulteen will try to set up a second meeting with the woman, perhaps another lunch. During this next meeting, he will pitch his proposition for sex.

Mistresses of Adulteens usually describe them as poor lovers because they're so focused on having their own orgasms; they're not concerned with pleasing a partner. Also, as maintaining a masculine image is so important to them, some Adulteens expect the woman to offer rave reviews about his sexual performance, thereby encouraging mistresses to fake the extent of their own pleasure.

How the Adulteen Relates to His Wife

The Adulteen does have an adult side to him. He willingly maintains a job and supports his family financially. This financial responsibility toward his family is often is reflected with love and admiration from the wife of an Adulteen. He enjoys his wife's respect and admiration and treats her better than he does anyone else. However, the Adulteen is likely to bridle at doing chores around the house and, at times, he will exhibit the insensitivity of a teenager in his behavior toward her.

The signature of poor communication and lack of openness in an Adulteen's marriage blocks any chance of real intimacy between him and his spouse. The Adulteen does not reveal himself to his wife or to anyone else, for that matter, and his wife's life typically revolves around events rather than around emotional intimacy. As a husband, an Adulteen will play the role of the boss in the family, all decisions being cleared with him to avoid his temper tantrums.

In most cases the Adulteen wants to keep his marriage and

makes an effort to maintain a proper family image in the community. Fitting with his portrait of being a hard worker, the Adulteen often hides his affairs under the guise of business meetings. His wife may or may not be aware of his affairs but, if she knows, she doesn't rock the boat.

As with the mistress, sex in the marriage is likely to be poor because the Adulteen is locked into a childhood view of all women, including his wife. Without openness and intimacy, how can sex be fulfilling? Consequently, an Adulteen's wife may fake her orgasms also.

Although the Adulteen does not feel a deep attachment to his wife, the couple will attend social functions together to maintain the all important appearances. Unless they know of his affairs, people will assume the marriage is good. Despite not being an emotionally thoughtful husband, he tends to be generous with things and, in many cases, his wife can have whatever material things he can afford. Generally, the Adulteen is successful in his career and both his achievements and his ability to support a wife help bolster his frail self-image.

Beware! Adulteens Brag to Their Friends

The characteristics of the adolescent phase, being mired in teen psychology, include a powerful need for peer group approval. Just as adolescent boys want to be seen as both popular and sexually successful so, too, do Adulteens. To keep up that image, the Adulteen shares the details of his affairs with his friends and brags about sexual conquests in the same way an adolescent boy would.

Adulteens Are Pals with Their Children

Adulteens often relate to their children as peers and any discipline in the family is likely administered by the mother. This is not because it's the easy way out for the father but because he enjoys being a pal to his child. Given the Adulteen's low self-esteem, its fragile nature being hidden from view, he avoids having it injured further by the criticism which might result if his youngsters saw him in the role of a restricting and inhibiting authority. This tendency toward being friends with the children is quite pronounced when his children reach their own teen years.

Many Adulteens re-live their adolescent stage again through their sons and daughters. The more self-centered the man is, the more he will want his children to reflect the image he wishes to present. He may stimulate, encourage and approve of aggressiveness and sexuality in his sons. In turn, some Adulteens are titillated by their daughters' sexual adventures and do not oppose this activity either.

What's wrong with the Adulteen's reluctance to serve as a parental authority? First, by removing discipline from the equation, the father deprives his children of the social education necessary during the transition from childhood to adulthood. Adolescents actually crave limits. They need to learn what is socially acceptable and what can harm them physically, emotionally and mentally before those threats become more dangerous later in life. Parental discipline generates self-discipline in the child, serving to promote achievement while protecting against the vagaries of life.

Both parents must be responsible for their children. The father who refuses to be an authority figure creates loopholes in children's moral standards and these loopholes generate a conscience that doesn't protect children from going down roads that are better left alone.

Being the pal and not the parent removes an important mature role model, particularly during the teen years. A son who witnesses his father's disrespect of his mother is destined to repeat those patterns in his own adult life. Immature fathers contribute directly to a lack of development in their own children. They transfer behaviors which may produce successful adults in some areas while denying their children the maturity in their personality to develop close, personal relationships.

Examples of Adulteens

Anthony

As communication had been nonexistent in his original family, Anthony was stuck in his adolescent years. Like his father, Anthony had buried his anxiety, vulnerability and sense of isolation under overwrought competitiveness. His father, a tough, muscular man, was himself competitive and their father-son relationship revolved around the ideals of masculine strength validated by winning. His mother quietly admired Anthony, the oldest of three sons, as her favorite child but Anthony saw his mother as inferior to his father whom he feared.

Constantly seeking his father's approval, while Anthony had his father's admiration, he also had his father's envy of Anthony's youth and achievement. Due to the envy and competition between them, it was not easy for the elder man to compliment Anthony or provide affirmation for his son's transition into manhood. As a teenager, Anthony couldn't win the physical battles with his father but he could vent his anger and frustration on his peers. He excelled in football, boxing and seducing the cheerleaders.

In adulthood Anthony enjoyed making the "big bucks" which demonstrated his power and social status. This Adulteen loved having people visit him with their "hat in hand" to entreat him to be on this board or that or to solicit him for donations. Anthony took delight in their deference to his opinions and their fear of his objections. Continuing his behavior pattern which began with cheerleaders, he racked up victories by bedding numerous women. His affairs varied in length from brief flings of a month or two to longer stints which might, as with Irene, last a year or so.

Like his mother, Anthony's wife, Julia, was a sweet, caring woman. Because he sensed his need for her as childish dependency and a threat to his masculinity, Anthony avoided closeness with Julia by diverting his attention to the affairs.

Jerry

When I first met Jerry, he was in his late forties. A bright and articulate man, he was working as a professor at a college outside New Orleans. Mimicking his students, Jerry usually dressed casually in T-shirts, jeans and tennis shoes. He had a beard, smoked heavily and drank. By the time of his therapy, he had been married to his second wife, Abby, a former student seventeen years his junior, for ten years. After a long history of affairs with his coeds and competitiveness with his male students which led to problems with the Dean, Jerry sought help.

This Adulteen enjoyed teaching and living out his role at the college. Jerry was a very popular teacher, attending many social functions and going on frequent walks or outings with students. Beginning early in his teaching career, the professor took advantage of the natural rapport with coeds in his class to start a series of trysts with them. In piecing the stories together, Jerry presented a pattern of engaging what he thought were competitive male students by making a point of trying to seduce the young men's girlfriends.

During an affair, Jerry could be engaging and fun. His courtship techniques were not all that different from a college student's. As with any college faculty member, Jerry's salary wasn't great, he didn't have extra money for dating and, in an arena where money was generally tight, coeds didn't have to be wined and dined.

Over a series of sessions, I learned more details about Jerry's two marriages. He met his first wife, Barbara, in college when he was a student. After graduation, they were married and he continued studying for a Ph.D. in American Literature. A daughter, Rebecca, was born two years after he became a professor. During the pregnancy Jerry began his extramarital affairs.

Then, when Rebecca was about 13, Barbara finally became suspicious. Jerry was inviting coeds to the house and, as Barbara could see, some of the relationships did not appear to be platonic. Jerry's wife expressed her anger and her desire for revenge by initiating an affair of her own with another member of the faculty. In a short time she fell in love with the other professor and decided to divorce Jerry to marry her lover. Within a year after his divorce, Jerry married Abby.

Jerry was happier in his second marriage and, yet, eight months later, he started an affair with still another student. A series of short affairs continued throughout his second marriage and Abby accepted this behavior, considering it part of Jerry's complexity and charm. She was in love with her husband and, from her point of view, Abby was happily married.

While Jerry held a tenured position and felt he couldn't be fired, he did carry out his affairs secretly, nevertheless, and became anxious when asked to the Dean's office for a conference. Despite his wife's love and admiration, the failure of his chronic affairs to permanently assuage his feelings of anxiety and unhappiness put him on a path which brought him to therapy.

Self-Help for the Adulteen

The Adulteen can return to his interrupted journey to maturity by taking an honest look at his life. Self-examination is both healthy and private. As you begin to understand your behavior and the limits you place upon your ability to embrace all of life, you will want to grow. At some point you may need to talk things out privately and a competent therapist is a viable option. In the meantime, here are some ideas to consider.

How would you feel if everyone knew about your affairs? If

these relationships became public knowledge and your veil of privacy were removed, would this contribute to your anxiety? If so, then you may well be playing teenaged mind games and operating with a teenager's logic. This immature reasoning involves doing things to prove your independence combined with a need to keep such activities secret.

An adult doesn't defy his own conscience and hide in darkness so a commitment to honesty with your wife and with others is an important step toward self-sufficiency. As you begin to learn healthy behaviors, the intimacy which makes life so much more rewarding will be possible. This will relieve the stresses which are driving your behavior as well as recovering the energy you are expending to maintain a false image.

Instead of hiding your feelings from your wife, just as a teenager might do with his parents, relieve yourself of the energy wasted in playing "hide and seek." Explore the potential for real intimacy with her through openness and sharing. Your wife may well respond by opening up to you. The two of you may then begin to take steps toward "clearing the air" and use the opportunity to move into a deeper level of discovery as you investigate the motives hidden in both of you.

What are your behavior patterns? Under what circumstances do they repeat? Are your emotional state and your attitude toward others similar to what you experienced during your teen years? Are your connections to people superficial and easily turned on and off? Do you have tantrums? Do you intimidate people with your behavior? Do you separate your marriage into one part of your mind while you engage in a sexual relationship with another woman? These indicators are consistent with the profile of an Adulteen.

Are you competitive at work, in your social life and in your sexual activity? While competitiveness can be an asset and, when you're successful, a source of pleasure, like too much caviar, being overly competitive can make you sick. Spreading competitiveness on every slice of life is a sure sign of an imbalance in your relationships. Competition can cause separation from others and, therefore, builds barriers between you and others. Being overly competitive as a way to achieve self-esteem is characteristic of adolescence.

What is the entire cost of your affairs? Are you aware of the risk to your marriage? Are you willing to accept emptiness and loneliness for the rest of your life? Look at your level of attachment to your wife and children. Is your connection to them superficial?

Adulteens tend to create superficial attachments typical of adolescence and these mean little and can be easily detached. In order to learn, teenagers experiment with their relationships and sample a variety of them. However, at this point in your life, well past the teen years, are you still experimenting in your links with women? Be aware that experimenting with sexual relationships can create a volatile and explosive situation within your marriage and can cause great hurt and harm if not a dissolution of your marriage.

If you're not the one with the problem, then who is? It's so easy to blame a spouse for our problems. The price is high, however, because blaming others creates a barrier to the real intimacy which is a natural part of a committed relationship. Are you prepared to make a commitment and to reap the very great rewards which flow from having a committed relationship?

Using falsely placed blame to support and to justify your extramarital fling is also a barrier to your own personal growth. The treadmill of affairs leads to orgasms, yes, but not to peace of mind. By having treadmill affairs, you sabotage any opportunity for true emotional satisfaction on many levels.

Being locked in troubled adolescence means giving up the security of becoming a mature adult who possesses the tools to take care of himself. It means continuing the dependence on other women for the fleeting pleasure of a sexual act. If your answer is:

"I like me as I am; I'd rather have sex," be prepared for a rocky road. The problems of life will force you to grow anyway but those lessons will be more painful because they will come later in life. By not dealing with your problems directly, you only compound the problems later.

Challenge yourself to developing intimacy with your wife through a total relationship with her, not just through sex. Everyone wants to have fun and to share laughter with a caring partner in a complete relationship. Any man or woman will eventually feel used and angry if their "significant other" only wants to be close during the time it takes to have an orgasm. A healthy marriage is more than a long term affair. Husbands and wives who are intimate can be "kids" together.

An emotionally secure adult can show the fun facets of his personality without fear of being seen as foolish, stupid or silly. That type of openness and the reciprocal acceptance of another person creates real intimacy. To only be playful with the "other woman" separates behaviors, robs your marriage of a vital element for enjoyment and doesn't give marital intimacy a chance for success. Make dates with your wife to do things you both enjoy. Be playful in your lives together. Fun in adult life is not just a luxury; it's essential. Play with the one who matters.

What does your wife need to know, if anything? As thoughtful as many books are on this subject, advice from experts conflicts and is often quite general. To answer this question, look to your goals. Do you want to hurt your partner, to dump your anger and anxiety on her and to create more distance between both of you? Or do you want to use the strain of telling her or, more likely, of admitting your adultery, as a beginning for building the relationship and moving toward a greater intimacy? Some marriages dissolve under disclosure while others find ways to work together with a new intimacy being their reward.

If you choose to talk, then the best approach is to limit the information to what is relevant but not sensational. For instance, the specific details of what you did in bed with another woman might add visual information to the sketchy picture your wife now has but this will only make her feel worse while pushing her to obsessively ask for further details. Anger and anxiety then whirls around like a destructive tornado. The pattern then repeats and builds, delaying or preventing healing.

While secrets and lies create walls between people, truth need not be stripped of consideration. Spend time getting to know your wife's attitudes, values, sensitivities and tolerance levels. Thoughtful truth will hurt but it has the best chance for eventual forgiveness. In time, if she recognizes the initial immaturity and the subsequent growth, then she'll see your communication as a sincere effort toward reconstruction, not destruction. Professional help may be exceptionally useful when navigating these shoals.

Build new friendships with married men who are monogamous. Use them as role models. We usually prefer to be with people who accept us rather than with those who would be critical of us, husbands having affairs will hang out with other men who speak their language, approve of infidelity, laugh at the humor in such escapades and show off the "other women" at private events which constitute a "No Wives Club." Monogamous men include their wives in their activities and, while they may not respond to your value system, thus adding to your initial discomfort, it is important for your growth to learn from them.

This reinforcement and approval of your affairs from your friends is actually of no help at all. An alcoholic who wants to go on the wagon doesn't hang out in bars. Along with all the psychological reasons, it just makes plain sense to seek others who will support your new behavior.

Adolescence has a place in our development but adulthood is a much more fulfilling place. Why is this so? Well, as teenagers, we're trying to fit all the pieces of our personality together. It's like playing with a jigsaw puzzle. We pick certain forms and try them in different sections of the picture. Sex is one of the pieces. Slowly, over time, we learn to share the important things we find with others. We learn to look beyond physical sex to emotional and mental intimacy. The desire for intimacy includes the full range of relating to someone you love.

In Woody Allen's classic movie, Annie Hall, there's a scene where a ghost-like image of Annie (Diane Keaton) leaves the bed and watches the sexual activity between herself and the Allen character, Alvy Singer. Annie isn't really there and she feels detached from the experience. There's no real intimacy. The experience can be summed up by the word "fucking" and every language has a term for it. Like Alvy, the Adulteen hasn't yet reached the next level of development where the sex part of the puzzle has been fit into the entire picture of an intimate adult relationship.

Survival Strategies for Wives of Adulteens

Although a betrayed wife will feel hurt, it's possible for her to continue to love a husband who has violated her trust. (This also holds true for a man who has become aware of his wife's affair.) If you suspect your husband of being an Adulteen, then it's important to see his "playing around" as the result of his own deeply seated personality problems. This isn't personal; he would have betrayed any wife, not just you. If shame is in the picture, then it is his, not yours. Remember, the Adulteen doesn't think he will be caught and usually isn't prepared for a divorce. Your attitude may well determine whether or not the marriage will survive.

Be resourceful. Survival for people and all animal life depends upon resourcefulness. How you deal with your situation will determine whether you will continue your emotional growth or be blocked by a barrier you, yourself, can't overcome. Nothing in life remains static, including your own emotional composition. As you and your husband deal with the current crisis, you can either grow or regress. Everything in life is in constant motion.

Food, drugs, alcohol or revenge, like affairs, are false activities to diminish stress. Tolerating stress is not easy for anyone, yet the ability to do so is a sign of emotional strength. Stay in touch with your feelings and with who you are while finding ways to relieve the stress. You might choose yoga and other forms of exercise, progressive relaxation, meditation and/or therapeutic breathing techniques. One of the best ways to lessen marital stress is to set aside time for open dialogue with your husband. Be patient. Due to his immaturity, your husband does not absorb nor does he process information accurately. Hints and nonverbal communication are not enough! Be direct.

Support from close friends or specific groups can be of great benefit. Avoid those who fuel your anger; you want to release the anger but without getting stuck in those feelings. Share the details of the story only with a close friend or two otherwise your social circle may not accept your husband back. Pick a confidant who has faced a similar situation and has succeeded in maintaining her marriage. Be wary of women who have divorced their husbands as they may be bitter and, thus, encourage your anger toward your husband.

Your philosophical or religious beliefs can be an anchor at times like this. In the long run, forgiveness will serve you better than turning to those who encourage your wrath, even if you divorce. The longer you are preoccupied with resentment, the more difficult it will be to get your thoughts clarified and organized. Obsessive thinking consumes time, time which becomes wasted in circular and nonproductive meditation.

Don't rush into a decision about your life and marriage while you're being driven by strong emotions. Give yourself and your husband time to discuss his behavior, the marital relationship and the feelings you have for each other. Then decide on a plan which feels right to you, first. A commitment to honesty is always a good beginning so an agreement to permanently put the lies and secrets aside is vital to any hope of reconciliation. This will inevitably expose you to his negative remarks and critical complaints so be prepared. Because trust must be mutual, avoid using the things he discloses against him. Attacking him will only trigger defensive mechanisms in his already fragile self image and could kill any movement toward growth. Healing the marriage will require a heavy investment from both partners.

Use this experience to learn more about yourself, your husband and others. There's much to learn from the bumps and pain of life. People often learn most about themselves during periods of change or crisis. During this challenging time, work on being truthful and open with your husband. Encourage the same openness in him. A marriage which is unable to handle the truth is already too weak to survive.

Even with the most favorable efforts, trusting will take a long time, as will complete forgiveness. If you're in a marriage troubled by the husband's infidelity, then know that he may be out of touch with his own problems. Exploring the issues can be an opportunity for growth both within the marriage and within each of you. Take time for reflection to review the entire relationship. Is this part of your life worth trying to save? If so, then make the effort.

Getting Back to Sex After the Shock

How soon should a woman resume sex with her husband after the discovery of his affair? There are no pat answers. Since people and relationships are so complex, the decision must be hers, alone, based upon her feelings.

Each wife will have her own sexual history as well as a developmental and earlier family history which adds to the complexity of the decision. Does this traumatic event awaken images of betrayals by a father or other men in her life? How much old baggage has been carried into the sexual reunion? How long will fears of rejection, abandonment and vulnerability dominate the intimacy?

Some people would say, "Go for it! Why deprive yourself of the pleasure?" They think the wife should take the risk and let her emotions catch up later. Those with this view don't trust time. The longer the wait, they think, the more distant, cool and anxious you both will feel.

Yet, while a wife may still love her husband, she might decide to wait until she also likes him again, for the friendship between them to be restored. It may be difficult for a couple to have satisfying, meaningful sex when waves of rage, distrust, guilt, jealousy and confusion are washing away the sands of serenity. Real friendship is a stronger bonding substance than lust, passion or even romance!

How Therapy Can Help

If a man can't work through personal problems on his own or together with the wife, then consideration should be given to the next step: help from a qualified professional.

The point of therapy is to shed light on the personality and behavior of the unfaithful man so he can understand himself. Hopefully the patient will use the insights gained from therapy to move from being an Adulteen to being a full, mature adult. Then, from this mature point of view, he can place new and higher values on his wife and their marital relationship. If the woman's personal problems are an issue in the marriage, then these can be explored as well.

Anthony After Therapy

Our first Adulteen was Anthony, the fifty-nine-year-old oil

company executive who was angered by his mistress's demands for marriage. In therapy, Anthony recognized that his affairs were hurting the "other women" and that he was not the victim of their wrath but, rather, the cause of it. Anthony also acknowledged that the affairs were stealing potential from the relationship with his wife Julia.

Because of an insensitivity to others, Anthony wasn't making the right connections in his mind. This man liked to think he was right and tended to look at everyone else as wrong or flawed. For Anthony to face his deficiencies as a person, husband and role model for his children was a blow to his already low self-esteem. Despite his falsely inflated ego, Anthony's underlying feelings of unworthiness were what threw him into the arms of the other women in the first place. For him, Anthony's acknowledgement of his flaws was an act of supreme courage.

Anthony had created a prison of narcissism which trapped him. On a deeper level, he did not feel secure enough to open up to the real intimacy of a loving relationship. As a result, Anthony was missing the fulfillment of loving another person as well as the nourishment to his character which flows from experiencing deep spousal love. Over time this Adulteen learned to open up to his wife and dealt more effectively with uncomfortable feelings and persistent problems. The affairs were eventually seen as a dissatisfying solution and other women were no longer pursued as Anthony grew up.

Jerry After Therapy

The second Adulteen was Jerry, a college professor in his late forties. Jerry was being soothed by his continuous affairs with a line of young coeds but this still didn't bring him peace. He felt anxiety and depression even though his second wife, Abby, found his affairs acceptable. Jerry was excessively driven by competitiveness with other men and vied with them for the attention of females. This reaction is ordinarily worked out in adolescence but not in Jerry's experience. He repeated the pattern continuously. The resulting conflicts only kept him agitated and discontented.

In Jerry's case his second wife Abby was an enabler, whereas his first wife, Barbara, had sought revenge by leaving him for another man. Jerry never expected his first marriage to end and he needed constant reassurance that his second wife, Abby, was happy and content.

In therapy Jerry recognized the repetitive patterns in his behavior; the dreams and fantasies which held him in his adolescence. Jerry's self-esteem improved when he incorporated his status as a professor with an image of himself as a responsible adult which was in sharp contrast to his earlier view of himself as a peer to his students. Becoming comfortable with being an authority himself came as a great relief to him.

CHAPTER THREE

Just Having Fun: The Playmate

Men deal with life
as children with play,
who first misuse,
then cast their toys-away.

– JOHN GILPIN, BY WILLIAM COWPER, ENGLISH POET (1731-1800)

A short, chubby, plain-featured man sat stiffly on the edge of the upholstered armchair in my office as he paused to puff on a cigarette. Looking at Larry, I thought of the few times I had encountered this forty-eight-year-old public relations executive at fund raising events. Although Larry had always been upbeat and friendly, now he seemed quite angry and defensive at our initial appointment. After clearing his throat, Larry continued his presentation, coming right to the point.

"Get this straight...I have no interest in giving up my fun with women," he said in an icy tone, "and I have no intention of getting into regular treatment with a shrink." Then, relaxing a little, Larry extinguished the cigarette and settled back into the chair. He had made the appointment under pressure from his wife, Bonnie, who was threatening to leave him if he didn't make the call. Larry looked into the distance for a moment before returning his attention to me. "Hey, don't take my lack of interest in treatment personally," he reassured me pleasantly, having bounced back to his usual cheery self. "Being in therapy just isn't my thing." Nevertheless, while he did his share of canceling and rescheduling meetings, Larry continued to make a new appointment at the end of each session.

Larry's lifestyle hadn't changed with marriage. He continued to enjoy playful encounters with various lovers and was living life as a playboy. Larry could well afford to court his lovers as he was an upwardly mobile "baby boomer" with a successful public relations business.

Though Larry was plain and overweight, he had a quick sense of humor and was extremely extroverted. He fit the so-called "Type A" personality: very active and aggressive but the aggressive behavior was well buffered with a sense of humor and a lively personality. He was fun to be around. Larry was a strobe-light character who people notice in a room; someone who shouts the message: "Hang around with me and you'll have a great time!"

In contrast to Larry, his wife, Bonnie, was strikingly beautiful, a former model now busy being the mother of four young children. Having a good-looking wife meant a lot to Larry and Bonnie shared this value in her appearance. After each child's birth, she had worked to get her figure back quickly with help from a personal trainer provided by Larry.

Although many pretty women are very bright, Bonnie wasn't one of them in Larry's eyes. Lacking interest in maintaining a close, intimate rapport with Bonnie, Larry did consider his wife to be beautiful but he "didn't marry Bonnie for her brain."

Larry saw himself as sharp with a big bank account to prove it and was worthy of attention. Larry complained about Bonnie being self-centered and passive in bed, wanting him to please her but not acting too interested in his satisfaction. He labeled Bonnie as a terrible lover who was mechanical and without feeling although this perspective was tempered somewhat by Larry's known reputation for sniping at others.

Larry sought out playful women to be his mistresses. He preferred lovers who would be seductive, flattering, fun-loving and available to travel on "business trips." In his line of work, Larry met many women and the idea of having a number of lovers seemed perfectly natural to him. Larry was so comfortable with playing around that, on one occasion when my late wife and I were walking out of a hotel lobby, he brought one of his mistresses over to meet us.

The Playmate Personality

Just as the Adulteen is easily spotted, you can also find adult children who exhibit the "Playmate" profile. Like a child, the Playmate emphasizes play in his life and he looks for opportunities to have fun throughout the course of his day. One of the Playmate's important playful activities is to have sex with diverse types of fun-loving women even though he will typically want to stay married. Larry fell into this category and, as you have read, he was quite attached to having sex outside of his marriage.

Why does the Playmate have a focus on play? Play provides an opportunity to absorb the many sources of anxiety that accumulate in life and both children and adults need to play, this being one reason for weekends and vacations. During play, we rearrange our experiences in our minds and are able to view them from different perspectives. We often work through problems in our thoughts while walking, biking, skiing or fishing. Play also helps us deal with deeper underlying problems as we explore our feelings and experiment with different behaviors. "All work and no play makes Jack a dull boy."

Unfaithful men who focus on finding playful women are

attempting to relieve their anxieties. For Playmates, affairs serve as a safety valve for many types of pressure. Since these relationships temporarily relieve anxiety driven pressures, Playmates become drawn to having affairs. There they find themselves entangled in the behavior by the immediate pleasure and the temporary escape, the reward affairs provide.

These adulterous relationships with playful women may also provide an arena in which Playmates can work through some of their own personal issues. As the motivating factors can be quite deep, this is not often done on a truly conscious level. For instance, during time spent with the mistress, the Playmate will revel in being the object of his partner, the recognition which he may have been denied as a child. He will relax and his thought processes will be stimulated to resolve personal issues.

Most Playmates avoid a life of hard work and responsibility. This eagerness for breaking their routine with play was reflected in comments made by more than one of these patients as we walked from the waiting room to my office.

Since I provide therapy to children as well as adults, I maintain a separate room filled with toys for treatment of youngsters. Upon passing the room, Playmates would ask, "Why do I have to talk all the time? Why can't I just have some play sessions like the children you treat?"

According to the Playmate profile, there's nothing wrong with "just playing around" with women; they're toys. Most of these men don't think of an affair as a betrayal of their wives. To them, playing with toys is just normal male behavior. Blinded to the issue of commitment, Playmates are driven by the desire to drain all the fun possible from life. As these men like eating, drinking and partying to excess, the Playmates I've seen are usually somewhat overweight. Disdainful of the discipline needed to keep in good shape, Playmates avoid gyms and fitness activity.

Playmates Without Children

While most of the Playmates I've treated were fathers, some were childless men. The involvement of children can differentiate between their behaviors. When a Playmate doesn't have children, he can carry out his playful affairs more easily. In those cases the man only has to contend with his wife and is much less concerned about staying married as his wife is only viewed as a more permanent toy. If his wife complains too much, then he'll seek a divorce and find a new long term toy.

Playmates who are childless may have a history of serial divorces and remarriages, easily having as many as three to five ex-wives. They are most likely to have betrayed every one of those women. Despite this, even if his new fiancee knows of the Playmate's history, the Playmate will pledge his fidelity without making the commitment in his mind. To gain the new bride's confidence, he will blame prior marital problems on the previous wives. Of course, after the wedding he will return to his previous patterns. Independent wives with high self-esteem will be more likely to end the faithless marriage within a short time.

How the Playmate Relates to His Mistress

The Playmate presents himself to his mistresses as a plaything for her, as an entertaining and fun guy who does not want anything serious. Depending upon the circumstances, he may or may not reveal his marital status. If the Playmate is in his own town, then he probably won't conceal his marriage because it's too easy to become unmasked. On the road, he'll be less forthcoming.

Playmates are usually not temperamental with their mistresses; they want them to see the relationship as fun and short-term. They tend to have Category One or weak Category Two affairs. Often Playmates will be generous with their mistresses but the generosity is seen in terms of buying the relationship. These men who want playful women will often talk about how much they enjoy hugging, kissing and the other games which precede sexual intercourse. Because making out and sex are key issues and because a Playmate is interested in a loving and responsive woman who will let him play out his fantasies, he will attend to her pleasures as well. The Playmate will seek out independent and intelligent women who have a good sense of humor.

The candidate mistress doesn't have to be attractive or have any particular physical attributes. Since he wants a woman who is fun and responsive to him, the Playmate puts aside any physical preferences. What the Playmate wants most of all is a woman who demonstrates joy and affection with being in his company. Just as in childhood when he could use play materials to gain a sense of accomplishment, a Playmate feels achievement when his mistress, his adult toy, accepts him.

Like the child who abandons the familiar toy for the new, the Playmate's affairs tend to be short-lived as the familiar mistress is replaced with the new. This is the result of a natural attachment that begins to form between the man and his mistress, a development the Playmate wants to avoid. In most cases, he doesn't want to threaten his marriage and will shut down his feelings for the "other woman," ending the affair to find another short-term diversion.

At the end of the day, a Playmate looks for a woman to join his play, not his life. He's not looking for commitment. In his mind, the type of woman he seeks will understand the rules of the game and know that when playtime ends, each person goes their own way.

How the Playmate Relates to His Wife

The Playmate's childish nature comes through in his demanding attitude toward his spouse. Typically, his mother treated him like a little king and he'll expect the same royal treatment from his wife. He may act like an immature dictator and become obsessed with having control over situations. Having a desire for attention, a Playmate is likely to throw tantrums when he feels his mate is not catering to him.

Playmates tend to marry women who are playful both in and out of the bedroom. However, if children start coming, then the marital relationship will start to weaken. A Playmate will not understand how demanding the role of mother can be and he will feel justified in seeking attention elsewhere. Having a working wife only adds to the competition which children bring and compounds the problem in the mind of the Playmate.

During our therapy sessions, the Playmates usually complained of inadequate or infrequent sex at home. Their wives had one excuse after another for avoiding sex and were mechanical and detached when they did engage in sex. The men didn't view sex as the most important aspect of marriage but rated it as a high source of potential pleasure.

Playmates who were fathers often cited another problem. Most conversations with their wives were serious discussions about the children and this frustrated the Playmates who wanted a more playful relationship with their mates. They didn't want to be reminded of their competition for their wives' time nor did they want to be reminded of their responsibilities. With his wife becoming a mother with duties, these men reacted negatively and looked for escapes.

Examples of Playmate

Larry

This Playmate was just a teenager when his father died. Although the family was very comfortable financially, his dad had paid the price by dying young from the workload he put on himself. Larry was driven by the possibility of an early death and, to avoid the mistake his father had made, he committed himself to enjoying life as much as possible. Larry wanted to die while playing, not while working.

Larry was a study in contrasts, although outgoing and friendly in business, he was superficial with everyone including his wife and children. Avoiding emotional intimacy, Larry frowned on openness and closeness. In Larry's home, his spouse did not have as many obligations as the typical Playmate wife because maids were present. Although Bonnie did not feel exhausted by the time Larry came home, the playful woman she once was had shifted into the mother role, a role which was made all the more difficult because her husband avoided the responsibilities and duties which came with children. Their romance and interest in sex dwindled on both sides. Larry soon started seeing other women for fun and excitement.

Larry was not experiencing pain in his lifestyle as he was practical in his approach to life. Out of touch with his underlying loneliness and anxiety, the superficiality which resulted was troubling Bonnie. She would complain about a lack of intimacy in their relationship but this complaint came as a mystery to Larry as he was taking care of all of Bonnie's practical needs. With limited awareness of intimacy within his own soul, he was unable to understand Bonnie's desire for intimacy. Bonnie felt insecure and very separate from Larry when she tried to discuss these feelings because Larry would react with anger and impatience. Since Larry's wife was the only mirror in his world which reflected flaws in his competence, Larry saw the complaints as stemming from Bonnie's own personal problems and he granted her wish to see a therapist.

In his premarital years, Larry had always had playful lovers and did not equate marriage with monogamy and intimacy. Like the typical Playmate, Larry was much more self-centered than the Adulteen described in the previous chapter. (In many cases, the Adulteen can be said to be a milder profile of the Playmate. Generally, Adulteens have phases of consideration and feelings for others; Playmates like Larry don't.) Larry was a Peter Pan who could fly out the window of family, work and responsibility and into a fantasy Never Never Land populated entirely by his pixy mistresses.

Sex with his mistresses made Larry feel alive, healthy, strong and attractive. His anxiety about a possible sudden death was diluted by sexual pleasure, the warm glow of many women and perpetual activity. As was mentioned earlier, Larry had the so-called "Type A" personality. In essence, his lifestyle of motion and delight gave him a feeling of euphoria and well-being, and being busy with a "full" life kept him from looking deeper into himself.

This Playmate enjoyed finding a new mistress at monthly intervals because he liked playing the game repeatedly from the beginning. The continuity of a relationship, such as in marriage, was not appealing to him. Each new playful woman and each new affair made Larry feel as if he had made a new start on life.

Most of the men in Larry's wide circle of friends were also having affairs. Their feedback and acceptance of his behavior rein-forced the positive image Larry wanted of himself. Because he had not been taught limits when he was a child, Larry did not feel guilty about womanizing. Anything he did had been fine his whole life.

Bert

By the time he came for a consultation, this thirty-nine-year-old middle manager for a respected oil company had been conducting light-hearted affairs for many years. Although Bert had picked a playful woman, Marilyn, for marriage fourteen years earlier, he felt she didn't communicate well. Over time, he began to see her as domineering and controlling. Nevertheless, Bert was not interested in divorcing Marilyn; he derived a certain level of comfort from being married.

His affair with Susan, a secretary in another department at the oil company, was typical of his pattern. Whenever he and Susan encountered each other in the building, they usually found something to laugh about and soon began to take time off so they could be together. Bert and Susan would spend hours in a hotel room where they did everything but have sexual intercourse. Bert felt comfortable with Susan and, when he was alone with his mistress, he could relax and have fun.

Bert's childhood had been filled with sadness. His father had deserted the family when Bert was still a young boy, forcing his mother to place her only child in foster care because she could not afford to take care of him. Through the eyes of a young child, this abandonment scarred him and left Bert with deep insecurities about intimate relationships.

As a young man, Bert had been very shy. He had married Marilyn because they were sleeping together and she had been good for him. She helped him to overcome his shyness and to strengthen his confidence. Later, Bert used playtime with the secretary, Susan, as a practice ground to give himself more confidence to move on to other playful lovers.

Bert gained a feeling of acceptance with each new mistress, a reward which he didn't find in his marriage. Then, when he felt his marriage had gone "flat" in comparison with his affairs, Bert turned to affairs as "spare tires," an alternate opportunity for play when he became disinterested in his wife.

Whether we look at Larry or Bert, we see men who assuage their emotional pain with laughter, fun and play. These men are bright, successful men who use women as playthings. All adults need play time for pleasure, to relieve tension and to stimulate creativity. The Playmate simply diverts this need for play into avoiding responsibilities of an intimate relationship. Sexual relief isn't essential in their affairs; playfulness is the critical element. Laughter and games consume the sorrow while the outward playful nature of these men is difficult for some women to resist.

Self-Help for the Playmate

Play with your wife once again. You married her because she was playful. If household chores, motherhood and/or career are demanding too much of your wife's time, then figure out ways to give her a break so the two of you can play. With more support from you, the two of you can create relaxing time together. Consider some of the following options.

- Hire a housekeeper to come in least once a week.
- Order a laundry service.
- Find a regular baby-sitter.
- Locate a grocery delivery service.
- As your budget permits, hire a tutor for the children, a handyman, a gardener, a backup cook, a pet groom or someone to run errands.

Any part of this list will be helpful; ask friends for referrals. You're also likely to find ways that you can pitch in with the chores yourself. Remember, some of the most common chores, when shared with someone you love, can become games in themselves.

Make dates with your wife; surprise her with nonsense. Give her a day at the spa before taking her out to a dinner, for a walk in the park or for a trolley ride. Surprise her with potted plants or mementoes which mean something only to you and her. Leave hidden love notes for her to find. Encourage her to find ways to make life more interesting while you put your own energy into pepping up the relationship. Why not do for your wife what you're doing for your mistresses?

Look at your motives and at what you really want. Your past history won't change but you can. Happiness and intimacy do not come from skillful sex and multiple orgasms. They don't come from having another person parrot back to you the responses you demand. You must become content with who you are, with yourself, which will require personal growth.

Why have you become dependent upon a string of mistresses to ease your anxiety over responsibility? If you focus on what's currently happening in your life and marriage, then you'll discover how you're using affairs to divert you from solving problems you can actually handle on your own and, usually, in a much more capable manner.

For those who don't learn to become self-sufficient in problem-solving, using others to solve their problems can become a well-worn pattern which, over time, only increases the insecurities and anxieties which flow from not being self-sufficient. If you give yourself a chance to find your own solutions, then you'll uncover your ability to be self-sufficient and, concurrent with this discovery, will come confidence, the antidote to anxiety.

Of course, change takes time and presents its own challenges, but overcoming the challenges which change will bring upon you results in new awareness and greater self-sufficiency. The increasing confidence in your own tested abilities will also make you more comfortable in your relationships. Nagging uncertainty will diminish, being replaced by stability and, quite simply, you will feel great.

How can you be a whole person while you scatter pieces of yourself everywhere? You're not giving up any of the pleasures of play if you bring them back into the relationship with your wife. More importantly, you actually retain the play in your memories as you recount them with your wife while you lose some memories every time another mistress departs. Reinforce your new behavior by associating with friends who place their primary priority on marriage. True self-esteem thrives in the self-image of honesty while living a life of deception kills the self-image. Honesty makes life simpler and simplicity in life is easier, less stressful, and more satisfying than living a life of deception. If affairs were the cure, then you would be healthy by now.

Take time to stop, to look and, especially, to listen to the people in your world. As a Playmate, because you use play to avoid pain, you are probably out of touch with your emotions which can also make you insensitive to others. A search for acceptance through affairs is a reaction to an inner loneliness. For this reason, in an effort to get attention, many Playmates are extroverts. However, they seem to have missed out on the maturation process which produces the ability to give and receive real love.

Being self-focused isn't the same as having self-acceptance and acceptance by others doesn't necessarily translate into self-acceptance, either. Reliance upon play for pleasure makes fantasy more important than reality and any relationship suffers. In solid relationships, two-way communication and empathy bring closeness where two way communication includes more active, attentive listening. Grow in your capacity to handle real emotional intimacy, the key to real happiness.

Survival Strategies for Wives of Playmates

After the shock and hurt, let the dust settle to prevent a mental paralysis which may prevent you from overcoming the challenges to your marriage. While the affair may be the result of his problems, you can be of great help if the two of you choose to move beyond the betrayal. Because all marital problems are complex, tackle one issue at a time. Be patient before deciding if the marriage is worth saving. Most of the time it is.

Over the past several decades more husbands have been confessing their affairs. However, when you learn of an affair, don't ask for details; just look at why he had the affair in the first place. What was he trying to accomplish? Your help will be invaluable if the marriage is to be salvaged. You can be part of the solution if his immaturity is understood by both of you.

Your husband can grow and bring the marriage to a higher level of emotional intimacy. However, in order for him to break out of his isolation, he's going to need your understanding and compassion. His affairs involved superficial relationships as he was looking primarily for play. Well, you can play, also.

Playfulness in sex is a private form of creative art. And, as in art, there are a wide range of expressions available. Lovingly shared sex with a familiar partner doesn't have to lose the excitement, passion and intensity found in earlier exploratory phases. Give more creativity and attention to this area of your relationship as play and creativity are important elements of sex to him as well.

Many Playmates can change but their wives must avoid sliding into the role of an enabler. While enablers love those they enable, their behavior prevents change. When Larry's wife, Bonnie, threatened to leave him unless he went for treatment, she started the growth process for Larry and for the marriage. Up to that point, she had been passively accepting the status quo in exchange for peace and comfort, hoping that age would magically change Larry. However, aging won't change the Playmate. What does work is changing the dynamics of the relationship. This sets the stage for Act II of the marriage rather than simply recycling familiar scenes from Act I over and over again.

Note that some wives of Playmates are simply bogged down with other responsibilities such as children or work and need to look for a balance of time for a husband along with the other demands in their lives. As your husband has sought relief in his affairs, are you seeking separation through dense activity? If the trouble between both of you is too much to carry, then seek professional counseling.

How Therapy Can Help

Larry

Engaging the Larry type of Playmate in therapy is difficult. A reluctant patient, unmotivated and unaware of what's going on in his head, such individuals often don't show up for sessions or they have a pattern of changing the times because therapy isn't play. Larry did miss appointments in an effort to protect his playground turf. Yet, over time, I was able to assist him in getting in touch with his anxiety, sadness and loneliness. Following my lead, he began an introspective journey.

Slowly, Larry connected his hidden expectation of a sudden and unpredictable catastrophe to his behavior in life. With this new awareness, Larry then accepted the uncertainty, realizing that he actually didn't have all the answers. This small shift in perspective opened onto a new road which led to significant progress.

Once his fears of a pending catastrophe were revealed, Larry was able to moderate his frantic search for pleasure. Eventually, the old motivation for having affairs just wasn't there anymore. His growth whetted his appetite for more introspection. Larry recognized that giving up his affairs were not taking away his pleasure; the change in behavior actually reduced the chaos and frenzy in his life and offered deeper pleasures still. Larry was hooked on discerning his real motives. From there, we worked on his devotion to hedonism and its connection to his pessimism. At first the only meaning in Larry's life came from making money. Then, when searching for other sources of meaning became important, Larry began to change as optimism permeated his attitude.

Larry began to enjoy his more relaxed pattern of living. He and his wife developed a greater intimacy in their relationship as they became playful again. Around that period in therapy, Larry told me of his closeness to Bonnie, a new experience for him.

Larry gave up serial affairs as a way of life and he was no longer a regular topic of local gossip.

Bert

Early in his childhood, Bert's family had been deserted by his father and his mother, unable to finance a household, placed her only child in foster care. As a result of being 'abandoned', at least in his eyes, Bert suffered from depression and an understandable insecurity about relationships. This mid-level manager for an oil company turned to playful affairs in an attempt to overcome his depression and his anxiety over being accepted. He also used affairs to relieve stress from his responsibilities in marriage and at work. Bert's affairs fell primarily into Category One or a weak Category Two.

Therapy helped Bert discover why he was unhappy in his marriage. With a little bit of effort and guidance, Bert learned to listen more and, in doing so, improved his communication with Marilyn. She responded by telling Bert about some of the unhappiness on her side of the marriage as well. Bert, himself, was shocked one day when Marilyn told him about an affair she had recently had. This revelation lead to an intense series of discussions between the two of them which stimulated both of them to work on staying together. The marriage between Bert and Marilyn continued and grew much stronger than ever before because both of them committed to making the marriage work. The problems became challenges they faced and defeated together and the furnace of the trials wedded them together much more closely.

By repressing his feelings and escaping to affairs for pleasure, the Playmate often squashes any real solution to his serious problems in relating to others. Therapy then becomes a model for communication. The pattern is then carried back into the marital relationship. Most of the men in this book created lifestyles which blocked communication and, in one way or another, poisoned intimacy in their marriages. Therapy seeks to teach honesty and communication, particularly the ability to listen, in order to deepen intimacy.

CHAPTER FOUR

Simply for the Thrill: The Pleasure Seeker

Enjoying things which are pleasant;
that is not the evil:
it is the reducing of our moral self
to slavery by them that is.

– ON HEROES, HERO-WORSHIP, AND THE HEROIC IN HISTORY,
BY THOMAS CARLYLE, SCOTTISH ESSAYIST,
HISTORIAN & SOCIAL CRITIC (1785-1881)

Carlos

This 35 year old family business owner arrived unhappy with the relationship he had with his wife, Debbie. After seven years of marriage, Debbie was refusing to have sex with Carlos most of the time. From his perspective, Carlos saw Debbie as a physically attractive yet cold, unaffectionate, controlling and demanding wife rather than, as is typically the case, simply responding to the immature view of intimacy Carlos offered. According to Carlos, Debbie was engrossed in caring for their two young children and, in many ways, Carlos felt that he was outside the family loop.

Again, this separation may have been a direct consequence of his Pleasure Seeker personality and the fantasies which were at work to protect his impaired self-image.

Typically, during the infrequent times when Carlos and Debbie did have intercourse, he was somewhat removed emotionally. Carlos was detached and would think about the same fantasies he had enjoyed during his teen years. Afterward, he and Debbie would argue when Debbie refused to role play in his fantasies. To avoid this scenario, Carlos usually turned to masturbation, an activity he had enjoyed consistently since adolescence.

A new family, a couple with three children, moved into the neighborhood. Debbie met the wife, Rose, at a yard sale and invited the couple over for an early evening dinner later that week. During the visit, Carlos enjoyed Rose's flirtatious nature. She even passed her work number to him while they were both getting drinks in the kitchen. The next day he phoned Rose and asked her to lunch. After several lunches and open discussions about sex, Rose said she was willing to act out the various fantasies Carlos had described. They started going to hotels and the activities they enjoyed related to the fantasies he had revealed to her.

His childhood was revealing. His mother, Vicky, was very attractive yet very insecure. She was dependent upon her husband, Roberto, the father of Carlos, who was bright and successful. As his parents traveled frequently, Carlos was raised primarily by a nanny. When he did poorly in high school, Carlos was sent to a private academy away from home. He managed to graduate but lasted only a semester in college before dropping out. His career was tied to an uncle's family business which Carlos purchased upon the man's retirement.

By the time I saw Carlos, he spoke of his hatred for both of his parents and kept his contact with them to a minimum. Apparently, his mother and father were locked into a "co-dependent" relationship and there was no room, nor had there ever been any room, for him in their lives. His mother's insecurity had been passed on when, in turning Carlos over to a nanny, her own immaturity had prevented Vicky from expressing love toward Carlos. Further blurring the role of his mother, his father, Roberto, acted as if he were a parent to his wife.

Debbie reflected the worst qualities of his parents as far as Carlos was concerned. He felt his wife was rigid like Roberto with the aloofness of Vicky. While Carlos never felt love from or toward his mistress, Rose, the pleasure she gave him passed as an acceptable substitute.

There were many other women before Rose. Carlos collected lovers from his business connections. Women responded to his quiet, nonaggressive tactics and they often volunteered to please him in his fantasyland. By being patient and quiet, Carlos avoided being accused of sexual harassment.

The Pleasure Seeker Personality

The Pleasure Seeker's view of sexuality is strongly oriented toward himself and for him masturbation is the most intimate form of sex. After all, with whom are you the most intimate if not yourself? For the Pleasure Seeker, the focus remains on himself even during sex in his marriage and in his affairs. He is engaged in masturbation rather than making love to his wife or his mistresses. His fantasies require the women in his life to be mere objects to be used to fulfill his dreams. For this reason, the Pleasure Seeker will literally use any part of a woman's body: her vagina, mouth, arm pits, breasts, hands, buttocks, thighs, etc., as a means of achieving physical satisfaction.

Pleasure Seekers have affairs throughout their lives and the sexual contacts with individual women range from brief encounters to extended ongoing encounters. These men tend to be promiscuous and callous with little effort expended in developing a relationship. Pleasure Seekers simply want orgasms achieved with women's body parts.

When sexuality remains embedded in the matrix of masturbation, women are viewed as mere objects for "autoerotic" activity. Thus, these men are indiscriminate. They don't really care if the object is bright or dull, attractive or plain, young or old. Of course, it's more exciting to him if she fits a personal preference in appearance or enjoys a favorite sexual activity but those demands are low on the priority list. Almost any woman will do.

Affairs involving a Pleasure Seeker are almost purely Category One, whether the man remains clothed or not. The capacity of these men to form intimate relationships is unusually weak because they harbor such strong self-centeredness and such an intense fear of closeness. Pleasure Seekers have a reduced ability to empathize and identify with others and this imprisons the man in childish, almost infantile, self-centeredness. These men may not even bother to arrange a date with a potential lover but, if they do, they want sex early. Sexual activity on a first or second date isn't uncommon.

One woman in therapy had agreed to a date with a Pleasure Seeker and was humiliated when they went out for dinner during their initial and only get-together. While at the restaurant, the man started pounding the table, shouting, "I want sex!" She was shocked and embarrassed and so were the other customers whose heads naturally swiftly swivelled to the unfortunate woman's table. Under normal circumstances, this intelligent and successful man was capable of reasonable behavior but was a complete prisoner so his sexual urges.

The desire to use any woman as a toy for masturbation is the Achilles' heel for these men. Lust distorts their judgement and their view of women as objects to be used for sexual pleasure work against any stabilizing force produced by empathy for their prospective partners. These men prey upon women, using any means available, and, at the same time, are vulnerable to the very risks and passions they accept.

How the Pleasure Seeker Relates to His Mistresses

The Pleasure Seeker doesn't have any deep attachment to either his wife or to his mistresses; he simply likes to have a woman available when he's interested in orgasm. To him, she's a body, possibly one he can use to act out his fantasies. Before he starts an affair, the Pleasure Seeker may often test the waters by revealing his fantasies to see if the woman is willing to participate in the activity. Then, during the affair, the man will be so focused on his own pleasure that developing consideration for the woman may seem like a distraction. Some Pleasure Seekers may be considerate, kind and somewhat romantic with their lovers, in keeping with their fantasies, but, no matter what, no promises are ever made. These men do not want to hurt or disturb their marriages.

The Pleasure Seeker likes to be the boss and the aggressor. He'll demand the upper hand in deciding the time and place for trysts and the conditions under which the two will become involved physically. The mistress has to accept the terms the Pleasure Seeker sets or the interaction becomes a one night stand. Any effort on her part to "call the shots" will not be tolerated because the Pleasure Seeker is managing his own fantasy and reality is precisely what he wants to avoid.

This man's dependency cannot be entrusted to any woman which, in turn, negates any intimacy. Moreover, the Pleasure Seeker may have a third and fourth mistress without anyone else knowing. A Pleasure Seeker known to me unintentionally impregnated the second mistress during a continuing affair with his primary mistress. Charming guy? Mistresses of Pleasure Seekers stand in the middle of a long line.

Some people call these men compulsive or sexually addicted due to the number and variety of affairs they have. The number of affairs reflects the depth of the Pleasure Seeker's pervasive fear of intimacy. These men seem to fear the "trap" of an ongoing relationship and a mistress will soon discover that her body, not her "soul," is the only drawing card.

How the Pleasure Seeker Relates to His Wife

The ability to be open, vulnerable and honest with one's wife just isn't there in a Pleasure Seeker. The couple will discuss everything about daily life except their "private" inner worlds. Yet the Pleasure Seeker, because he equates sex with intimacy, will see sex with his wife as the expression of intimacy. A Pleasure Seeker and his spouse may have sex often, regularly or occasionally, however, it will revolve around the mechanics of sex, not the intimacy of a real emotional relationship. These marriages tend to be intellectual and sterile.

Just as he views everyone else, the Pleasure Seeker sees his wife as merely one of the "things" in his world. The Pleasure Seeker, in attempting to maintain his individuality, authenticity, freedom and self-sufficiency through his fantasies actually sacrifices these elements of a healthy psyche by avoiding closeness. Because his narcissism is so deep and so prevalent, a Pleasure Seeker doesn't respond to, nor does he employ, the emotions and communications associated with true intimacy.

A wife who stays with a Pleasure Seeker may accept her husband's patterns because they fit her own low comfort level in attaching to another person emotionally or because some other aspect of her own agenda compels her to do so. Other wives in this situation are less aware of her husband's immaturity. They may simply accept the marriage as typical and forego any search for a deeper and more intimate relationship with him. In still other cases, a healthy wife with more discernment may become depressed, exhibit rage at the Pleasure Seeker and/or turn to alcohol or drugs.

The Pleasure Seeker won't fight back when his wife is critical as he ascribes her outbursts to events unconnected to him or as changes in hormones or general emotional instability. A Pleasure Seeker's wife may refuse to have sex with him for a while in an attempt to force the man to change or she might take a lover of her own out of revenge. Life with the Pleasure Seeker can be its own hell and Pleasure Seekers are difficult to reach and motivate.

A Closer Look at the Issues

While, in the normal course of development, masturbation may serve a purpose, it can become a problem if the man doesn't mature and views women as merely an accessory to masturbation. This describes the basic flaw in the Pleasure Seeker and explains why he isn't able to relate to women in an intimate way, wife and mistresses alike, when making love to them. The Pleasure Seeker's use of women as objects for masturbation reflects his lack of vital developmental progress in social attitudes as he moved through adolescence into adulthood. As the Pleasure Seeker retreats into his fantasies, he reveals unresolved conflicts from earlier periods in his life and the defense mechanism of fantasies block real intimacy with another adult.

In a healthy relationship, intimacy is a multi-layered experience signified by the layers of a wedding cake. It includes an openness with feelings, an honest sharing of experiences, a trust in not being hurt, a closeness in sexual expression and mutual acceptance. However the Pleasure Seeker looks at the top physical layer of the cake, the small layer, and sees the mantle as intimacy. He will become confused and angry if his wife doesn't want to have sex on demand. He'll think she's avoiding intimacy with him and will interpret her refusal as rejection.

As the Pleasure Seeker uses sex as a window into his self-worth, acceptance as a sexual being reinforces his self-esteem, whether the validation comes from his wife or a mistress. Therefore, any unavailability from a partner or her refusal of sex stirs feelings of insecurity in the Pleasure Seeker. In contrast, mature people are more strongly integrated in their personality and are able to relate to others without constant reaffirmation of their esteem. Even more importantly, because of their maturity, these adults aren't threatened by openness or closeness and, with more of the wedding cake available to be explored, they can give a more honest, complete love to another person. Even healthy relationships are not necessarily free of anxiety and stress but the level of maturity which is present allows those feelings to be identified, handled and managed. These qualities are absent in the Pleasure Seeker.

Examples of Pleasure Seekers

Kurtis

Although this unhappy 42-year-old Pleasure Seeker made good money, Kurtis knew his job as a foreman at a New Orleans shipyard was going nowhere. The same was true with his marriage. He didn't feel close to Camille, whom he had married ten years earlier. His wife was a full-time mother who kept busy with their three young children.

In our meetings Kurtis came across as a bright, likable diamond-in-the-rough. He was tough and husky with good features. Impatient with frustration, Kurtis demonstrated a short fuse. He was a heavy smoker and a binge drinker unconcerned about his health.

Throughout his years with Camille, Kurtis had maintained an emotional distance from his wife. He came home, ate dinner, watched sports on TV, drank beer and went to sleep early. At times he had sex with his wife but, usually, Kurtis turned to solitary masturbation. Kurtis liked having his penis between Camille's breasts and enjoyed manual satisfaction, activities she saw as being "weird," consequently, sex between them was infrequent.

Because of his tendency to be sullen, Kurtis kept Camille on edge and continually worried about his moods. She walked a tight rope between his outbursts. Camille was a good, concerned and involved mother but Kurtis was the boss of the family where he wanted to be boss. He controlled the finances and took care of repairs to the house while the children were primarily left to Camille.

Several years before beginning therapy, Kurtis had encountered a married waitress, Nicolle, at a restaurant near the docks and was immediately attracted to her large breasts. Though he couldn't meet Nicolle regularly, with various creative deceptions, they managed trysts together over several years. Putting her hands and breasts to good use, she liked doing the things they did in bed as much as Kurtis did. In control of their relationship, he decided when and where they would meet and Nicolle was usually agreeable.

Intercourse was not Kurtis's goal. Nicolle's large bosom was important to him because Kurtis liked rubbing his penis between her breasts while he squeezed them together. He also did the same with her thighs and enjoyed masturbating while Nicolle did the same for herself. As Nicolle was a perfect partner, their relationship lasted longer than most Pleasure Seeker patterns. Yet this relationship fit mostly into a Category One profile. There wasn't much emotional intimacy on either side and even when Kurtis had fantasies of marrying Nicolle, it wasn't in terms of loving her but in terms of fantasies which reflected how well she fit into his fantasies. Kurtis was clearly focused on masturbation.

Kurtis also enjoyed pornographic movie emporiums where he would masturbate in a booth. However, Kurtis worried about these places being raided and his subsequent arrest which he feared would lead to him being fired. Kurtis also liked to masturbate in unusual places such as department stores; the risk excited him.

When Kurtis was just seven his mother died and his father

remarried. Feeling abandoned while growing up, Kurtis kept some distance from his father and stepmother. Meanwhile, he became angry with his mother for dying and leaving him. Later, this pent-up anger and sense of abandonment was directed toward his wife. If Camille went out for something so common as an evening of cards with her girlfriends, then it would be sufficient provocation to trigger his feelings of abandonment.

Once, before his mother died, Kurtis had seen his mother and father making love. These images of his mother were seen by Kurtis as being loving. In his teen years, mental pictures from this episode were incorporated into his masturbation fantasies and, later, as an adult, Kurtis viewed women who would act out his fantasies as being ideal. Those women who wouldn't, like Camille, were considered cold. Thus, he justified the "loving" affair with Nicolle by contrasting her with his wife who, as a "frigid" woman, didn't really love him.

Pleasure Seekers-like Carlos and Kurtis focus on masturbation as a means of maintaining self-control, self-sufficiency and a way of relieving unhappiness and stress. Men in this pattern may appear to be engaged in the same sexual behavior as a loving partner but their thoughts scroll through favorite masturbation fantasies. Sex with a Pleasure Seeker is sure to offer only short term satisfaction.

Self-Help for the Pleasure Seeker

Is your focus in sex rarely about intercourse? Intercourse doesn't have to be a goal in every sexual experience, but you may be a Pleasure Seeker if the goal is to be rubbed into an orgasm.

Are your sexual fantasies similar to the ones you had in your teen years? Think about your favorite fantasies for excitement. Have they remained fairly constant since your teen years? Having "old" fantasies isn't unusual but when you put it together with a "yes" to the previous question, the pattern for a Pleasure Seeker begins to form.

Do you remain emotionally detached from your mistresses? When sex is the goal of the relationship and you don't want to be involved with another's life, you're not in a real relationship. Although your mistress is human, is she just a device, an inflatable doll, to be used for physical gratification?

Is your experience when making love in and out of your marriage similar to masturbation? When your focus is on you, even normal intercourse can be a form of masturbation. Making love involves a relationship and two way emotional intimacy. Masturbation is centered on the self and does not involve two way communication or intimacy.

Is there a repetitive and compulsive nature to the sex you enjoy? Everyone has preferred patterns in sex and then variations for new excitement. In contrast, finding new partners for the same patterns reflects the masturbatory profile. Serial partners for the same repetitive activity is an extension of the earlier masturbation. In masturbation variety is supplied by new partners not from the variety provided by intimacy.

Do you block emotional attachments to your wife? It's human to bond when there is regular contact with another person but a real relationship can exist only when the partners continue to grow as individuals within their association. Fostering growth in a marriage includes a loving, concerned awareness and acceptance of your wife's needs. Avoiding closeness in your marriage doesn't give either of you a chance for a successful, fulfilling life.

Self-help starts with insight. If you realize that you're viewing women as sex toys, then start building the relationship that has been missing with your wife. Look her in the eyes when making love. Increase your awareness of her as a person. Ask questions about her feelings. You'll know you're in a real relationship when the lovemaking becomes more intense than ever and the mechanics are no longer the issue.

Survival Strategies for Wives of Pleasure Seekers

Most women easily recognize when sex is mechanical. Masturbatory sex lacks the intimacy of making love. Is this the quality of the sex that you and your husband have? If so, it's time to build more intimacy into your marriage and sex life. Here are some points to keep in mind as you work on your relationship.

If you can see Pleasure Seeker patterns in your husband, by all means tell him. Let him know. You both have work to do on changing your sex into a more intimate, emotional experience. Draw on his fantasies. After all, he is competent in creating them. He just needs new ones.

Create some suggestions if the sex has become boring and predictable. A disruption of the mechanical routine will help break your husband's compulsive pattern. If you need ideas, then see the additional reading section at the end of this book.

Playing out his fantasy is fine if both of you enjoy it and if no one is being hurt. Remember, though, that you don't have to participate in acts which are not emotionally acceptable. If there's a problem, then talk it over with your husband when you're not in bed.

The issue is not really the mechanics of sex; it's how you feel and relate to each other. Focusing on just the mechanics is not going to give the rewards of fulfillment. Openness, honesty, communication, tenderness and helping each other reach the next level bring the rewards of real intimacy. Helping another person to grow and develop brings huge rewards to both partners.

Think about how to teach your husband to see you as a real person, not as a toy. Be your own person. Hold on to who and what you are. Have and display a sense of self. Express your self-respect, self-worth, identity and your inner security about who you are.

The bible tells us to "Love your neighbor as thyself." The saying has deep significance for intimacy as it assumes an improving, healthy self-love, self-worth and self-esteem in one person can be shared with another as both partners mature. A continually growing sense of self-value then plays itself out in relationships. When self-regard is not healthy, it is defensive, grandiose and destructive. Cold-blooded killers often hate themselves and, as these people do not value their own lives, they can't empathize and value the lives of others!

Exposing your inner feelings without asking for agreement can produce anxiety but it can strengthen the intimacy of your relationship. In turn, your husband will feel less obligated to mask his true feelings and less threatened by disagreement. He will feel your security and be encouraged to be his own authentic self as well. These steps begin the journey toward expressing mature love.

If he responds to your help, then you will feel it. Trust your intuition, your feelings. Yes, his affairs with other women were serious breeches in the marital bond and his betrayal will be tough to accept but life is short. Put in the time necessary to regain the lost connection if you want your marriage to continue. The affairs were not emotional investments for him and the other women were just toys for masturbation. Now that he is working on discovering you as a person, find ways to make sex a loving experience. Have fun, enjoy the adventure of showing your husband a whole new emotional world. Take him down through the layers of the wedding cake. Both of you will notice the difference and, together, you can enjoy the discovery.

The wife who understands that the cause of the infidelity is a problem within her husband and not within herself can help in various ways. If more assistance is needed, therapy is recommended. A marriage involving a Pleasure Seeker can be saved if both parties agree to put in the effort and see eye-to-eye on the goal but this is a particularly challenging goal to achieve with this profile without guidance.

How Therapy Can Help

Carlos & Kurtis

Through therapy, both Carlos and Kurtis saw their masturbation fantasies during sex as tell-tale signs of their immaturity and anxiety. While struggles for independence from a mother are normal during development, for Carlos and Kurtis this continued to be fueled by unresolved anger and guilt and were then transferred to their marriages when they became physical adults. Both Carlos and Kurtis avoided emotional intimacy because it was seen as a threat to their independence. The low-key affairs were a way to divert intimacy from their marriages and permitted them to remain separate. Thus, by staying emotionally detached, Carlos and Kurtis felt safe, independent and in control of their identities. However, the anxieties continued, as did the guilt and anger, because the affairs were only a temporary balm for the real problems.

Therapy helped both of these men recognize the connection between their personal history, their current mental state and their behavior. Men like to solve problems and when Carlos and Kurtis saw the meaning of what they were doing in terms of a problem to be solved, it was a "Eureka!" type of discovery. The two men were able to opt for change.

Eventually, in the course of therapy, Carlos and Kurtis each terminated their affairs and they felt much less pressure to convince their wives to act out fantasies. Both began to see their spouses as people, as something more than objects for masturbation, and, as a result, the marriages moved on to a more intimate relationship.

CHAPTER FIVE

High on Conquest: The Conquistador

---

*Is there anything in life
so disenchanting as attainment?*

– "THE ADVENTURE OF THE HANSOM CAB," NEW ARABIAN NIGHTS,
BY ROBERT LOUIS STEVENSON, SCOTTISH AUTHOR (1850-1894)

The men who "go to war" against women, who manipulate and seduce them, consider it a display of manhood. To the contrary, the need to validate their manhood by conquest merely exposes their boyhood. The deceived and vanquished women, like all victims of aggression, can become vengeful ....

George, a successful attorney in his mid-fifties, was the target of such a woman. Frustrated by threats by his angry twenty-five-year-old mistress, Margot, George wanted a solution. Margot, a court reporter, was threatening to make their affair public. A local judge who had sought therapy for a drinking problem sent George to me. George wouldn't have been in therapy if he "wasn't sweating over the Margot situation."

"At this stage in my career, my friends in politics feel I should run for public office. I have all the connections and surveys show strong support within my district. While people seem to accept the affairs of politicians, I'd hate to risk having this one get into the news. I've had a lot of affairs so it could get ugly. You know, if the public knew all the facts about the guys they've elected, then there would be a lot of empty seats under the Dome. It would be crazy for me to try to cope with an angry wife, confused children, a law practice and the election all at the same time."

"Margot loves me and wants a family," George said. "She wants me to get a divorce and marry her. However, I've told her more than once that I wasn't looking for another marriage. Previous to this one, I had a marriage when I was in college and had a child by my first wife. I'm in my second marriage now and it has lasted almost 15 years. We have two young children and I don't want more of the same with a third wife. My wife Norma and I get along fine."

George had first noticed Norma back in his college days. He described the Norma of those days as "a beauty queen who was quite popular." Their initial meeting followed a collegiate golf tournament in which George had done well. About a month later he managed to sleep with Norma before she found out about his wife, Jenny, and his young family. (Norma had seen George with Jenny and his daughter at a local restaurant.)

"Norma was disturbed but we kept seeing each other," George said. "Within a year, I divorced Jenny and, two years later, married Norma. Yet, while I was dating Norma, I couldn't resist going after a girl in my study group at law school. The study group was impressed with Vanessa. She made the Law Review. I didn't; but I made her."

Vanessa was married now "but not to a lawyer" and she always acted "cold" when they bumped into each other at social gatherings. George didn't understand Vanessa's attitude since she had been a "willing party" to their affair. "Why is her nose out of joint?" he wondered. "I lost interest in her after a few weeks and she switched out of the study group. I was relieved to not be seeing her twice a week in such a close environment."

The Conquistador Personality

One of the most common types of philanderers are the Conquistadors who are identified by their competitive nature and their drive to win at everything. Both men and women recognize this profile readily and know the affairs flow from a need "to make a conquest." In other words, the men are more interested in "Scoring" than they are in a relationship. In fact, a relationship with the woman is not even on the table. The game is about winning and losing.

The Conquistador personality displays a high level of aggressiveness mixed with extreme self-centeredness. These men have a diminished capacity for empathy and commitment. Both their wives and their mistresses are merely trophies.

The Conquistador's value system is immature and he places great emphasis on the celebrity status, wealth, power, physical beauty, family origin, etc., of the woman he targets. Who the woman is as a socially desired object will be more important than who she is as a person. Conquistadors are not looking for just any woman; they want THE woman, the best. The wife of a man whom the Conquistador admires can be a choice target because sleeping with the wife of a powerful man adds to the sense of victory against a worthy opponent. In his mind, the seduction of a trophy woman signifies ownership.

One conquest is never enough. As envy is an important driving force in the conquest, as there are always men and women to envy and, as the affair devalues the target and her other associations, the same pattern is continuously replicated. Once the next affair becomes established, the Conquistador, in his drive to be superior, finds reasons to fault his mistress. In due time, he will think of her as "ordinary." His self-esteem will temporarily improve as the victory is gained and it becomes his option to discard the woman. Dropped and labeled as "no longer desirable," the mistress will experience corresponding damage to her self-esteem.

Conquistadors have strong feelings about their social image and they aren't inclined to become guilt ridden. Conquering women is only one of many stepping rungs in the climb up the social ladder. As far as these men are concerned, they're not doing anything harmful or wrong and become concerned only when exposure is a possibility. Their targets will be women who are active, consenting partners.

How the Conquistador Relates to His Mistress

In constant need of affirmation, the Conquistador experiences mood swings and irritability when his measures of status come under attack. As a result, his affairs will often be brief. Although the affairs can be glamorous and exciting, they will also be superficial and, when the victory has been attained, the present mistress will be left for a new affirming conquest. The flame burns brightly but it also burns quickly. These men keep a certain distance from their mistresses and clearly state their lack of serious interest in any relationship with a woman. When she hears the Conquistador openly limit the extent of the relationship, the mistress would be well advised to pay attention.

As his interest begins to wane, considerate thoughts and actions will decrease. Becoming critical, the Conquistador will see the faults of his mistress instead of the qualities which originally attracted him. Like the euphoria after a victory in a big game, the excitement he once felt passes. Mistresses are left bewildered and confused as the intensity, passion and romance, the sparkle and glow of the affair, quickly goes out for him even while a bright flame burns in her. His pleasure comes from the chase and conquest, not from the relationship.

The Conquistador's affairs vary in duration from a few weeks to maybe a year or so. However, the longer the relationship survives, the more the affirmation diminishes as ownership sets in. Mood swings reappear and the purpose for the affair is no longer fulfilled. The dominating side of the conquest type man becomes increasingly apparent. Due to his aggression, he will be prone to temper tantrums. In some cases, the aggressive Conquistador may even become sadistic with his need for control possibly being expressed by violence.

How the Conquistador Relates to His Wife

The Conquistador is exploitive. He doesn't invest his emotions in anyone, not even his wife. The marital relationship is not much more intimate than the one with the mistress of the hour. He won't be honest and open with his wife in any of their interactions including their sexual relationship. These men manage anxiety poorly and do not have the internal strength to soothe themselves in times of stress. Consequently, they rely on others to reassure them. Curiously, while Conquistadors don't offer love or loyalty, they demand everything from others and, as a result, their marriages deteriorate over time.

More often than not, his wife eventually reaches a point of no return and leaves him. However, since social appearances are important to both, these couples often maintain a good front and their friends will be surprised at the news of a pending divorce. As the aggressive nature of the Conquistador makes him a good provider, it can take ten to twenty years for a Conquistador's wife to give up when she eventually sees herself as an earlier conquest in a devalued marriage.

Even when the Conquistador makes the decision to divorce his current wife to marry a new conquest, his behavior in his new marriage won't be different over the long run. In time, the new bride will be discarded for new conquests as the demeaning and devaluing behavior of the Conquistador recycles.

Men Who Seek Conquest

Look over the history of humankind and you will see evidence of the hunter mentality in the human species. Even today, men are still drawn to the challenge, excitement and ecstasy of hunting which is expressed in modern forms of love, play and work. For some males, the taking of a single wife doesn't satisfy their emotional hunger in the romantic arena. Hunting season comes frequently as winning a new prize provides a temporary, stabilizing fix. In time a new season arrives and the need for another conquest to ease the soul will reappear.

A man engaged in conquest comes armed with a quiver of deadly arrows. A Conquistador will be aggressive, passionate and consumed with the chase. The target, always a gem among women, will think she has generated his passion and is prone to being "swept off her feet." A woman who responds to this passion with early sex will find herself in bed with "a stranger." Women are just another notch on a scoreboard. The Conquistador has no remorse nor any concern about his actions as he moves on to the next target.

The Conquistador's aggression, like the Black Hole of outer space, sucks away the qualities necessary for a mature relationship. Moral commitment, a sense of responsibility and ethical values are destroyed. He uses "love" as a pretense to gain control and power over women. Lacking a strong interior core, the control the Conquistador demands is woven into a false sense of security and is a form of self-protection.

Examples of Conquistadors

George

George's father, Albert, wanted his son to be tough. To make him tough, Albert would put boxing gloves on George and deliberately hurt the young boy to teach him "how to take a punch."

From this, George learned to be an aggressive bully in school.

In contrast to his father, George's mother was a passive, doting woman who indulged her son's every wish. This firstborn of three sons, as his mistresses would discover, became quite skilled and cunning in manipulating women into giving him what he wanted.

George was three years older than his closest brother, Dan. These two siblings were very competitive with each other and fought into adolescence. In manhood the two became buddies although neither had much of a relationship with Jimmy who was eight years younger than George. The older boys teased Jimmy about his lack of interest in sports and his quiet, passive demeanor. In adulthood, Jimmy announced his homosexual orientation and now keeps his distance from the men in the family.

Earl

This fifty-two year old Conquistador suffered from depression. He had worked for the same insurance agency for two decades, an agency started by his grandfather. Earl was a company officer, married for twenty-one years with three daughters. Earl was also having an affair with Cynthia, a married woman from a prominent local family whom he met at a social event during Mardi Gras. Earl said he didn't feel guilty about his affair; he openly gave me the facts.

Earl regretted being married but loved his daughters. Before Cynthia, Earl had been involved in an earlier affair which his wife, Monica, discovered. She then shared the news with their three daughters. The oldest became troubled but the two younger daughters were unconcerned. In keeping to the pattern, the affair was with a popular, beautiful amateur actress from a local theatre company.

"These are not ordinary women," Earl emphasized. "They are dynamite! Any man would be happy to be in bed with any one of them. I'm very attracted to women who are doing their own thing in the world. Maybe I'm just reacting to their vibes."

Earl said he was losing interest in Cynthia whom he'd been seeing for over a year by this time. Again, true to pattern, Cynthia was becoming too demanding and the relationship was starting to be "too much trouble." Continuing with the pattern, Earl was "getting ready to go after someone else."

" There are a lot of attractive women in New Orleans and my wife, Monica, is one of them. There's really nothing wrong with her. Maybe she's a little overweight, but not bad. While people tell me how attractive she is, I still have a hard time getting excited about her. With the other women, sex is great. But with Monica, I have to take Viagra."

Exhibiting the typical pattern of complaint with those who are too close, Earl said he wanted his wife to get a job but she thought the girls needed her at home. "What really gets to me is the way she argues about my opinions and decisions. She's very competitive and we end up quarreling about everything. She says I'm too critical of her and the children. When I want sex, we have sex and it relieves the tension for a while. At least until the next day. Then she'll accuse me of being rough and cold."

Although Earl said he was a member of a few social organizations, he considered himself to be a loner. His one sense of belonging came from his time in the Army Special Forces. He enlisted after college and became a lieutenant. "The training was tough but I did well in the one-on-one fighting drills," Earl remembered. "Successful men know how to compete and win." Being accepted into this group had reinforced Earl's confidence in his masculinity. He remains nostalgic about those years to this day.

Earl's father also worked in the family insurance agency. "We've never been close," Earl admitted. "I'm much closer with my mother and usually avoid dealing with my father. There are times when I do need his assistance and he is always helpful but I think he might be a loner also."

Self-Help for the Conquistador

We all have emotions and the truly masculine man is comfortable both with having emotions as well as with the emotions he does have. The immature man, because his emotions confuse him, denies his emotions which leads to isolation followed by any number of self destructive behaviors. Reaching out through aggressive womanizing is one of them.

We all have anxiety but the difference between the healthy person and the immature person can be seen in how they handle anxiety. The mature person faces the anxiety and gets to the source. The immature person runs from the anxiety and hides himself in diverting activities. Thus affairs are diverting and a sign of immaturity. A deeper self-awareness will begin the journey to correcting the destructive behaviors which are being expressed by aggressive gestures toward women. Note the thoughts you have when you feel anxious. What are their sources? Are the fears reasonable? Challenge the thoughts and think them through. Then move your thoughts toward positive actions you can take to gain control of the issues which are surfacing.

We all have limitations; it's human. We can't fly so we build airplanes. We can't carry heavy loads so we build trucks and trains. We can't run great distances so we build cars. Humanity has a history of overcoming limitations. Limitations aren't a sign of weakness; limitations are problems just waiting to be solved. Conquistadors who focus on aggressiveness as a show of masculinity and strength do so to cover their limitations and, in doing so, turn the limitations into weakness because the problems are never solved. It takes a full self-awareness to grow and change.

All of us need other people. We're designed to be individuals in a social setting. Men who target "special women" as trophies exploit and destroy the social setting by attacking the bonds which hold people together. This inappropriate aggressiveness is a cover for the natural limitations which are basic human needs. To overcome our limitations we must rely upon others. Conquistadors see this interlocking dependence as a weakness when, examined more closely, the interdependence is actually a solution to a host of limitations.

Boosting self-esteem or self-confidence from conquering a "celebrity" is a trap. The very need for conquest betrays the reason for the conquest. The true source of emotional growth and nourishment is from honest, intimate relationships. Trivializing another person, deceiving them and then discarding them after they have been used does nothing to build self-esteem or strength. The repeated pattern of conquest only sows the seeds for more conquest and, as each conquest fades, the anxiety returns and the doubts require another conquest.

Look at your role models and the lives these people live. Are they content, are they happily married to their first wife, are they stable? Or do your role models present a false front to hide an underlying sense of weakness, inferiority, shame and unworthiness? Thinking about the behavior of these models and the results they obtain can help you identify the roots of some of your own unproductive patterns and the long term consequences you should expect if you continue in those patterns.

Give more attention to your wife, family and community. Take an interest in your spouse and in your children. Find out why they like doing what they do by doing what they like to do with them. You may also find more mature, male role models doing what makes men men as you join the fun.

Look in many parts of your world for healthier models of masculinity. How do other men direct their aggressions into healthy activities? While aggression is a natural feature of the masculine man, using that aggressiveness productively is a feature of the mature masculine man. Funneling aggression into socially beneficial occupational or humanitarian endeavors can be very satisfying.

How do you relate to your wife and to your mistresses? Domination leaves no room for true intimacy and, ironically, a need to attain superiority over women denotes inferiority. Find activities which reinforce positive feelings about yourself. This could be a company softball team, volunteering in Habitat for Humanity or a home remodeling project or a new family activity. As you grow in confidence and as others begin to acknowledge their appreciation, you'll find the connection to your wife strengthening as well.

It is necessarily important to accept responsibility for what you've done. Don't be defensive; we all make good decisions and we all make bad decisions. Then, as you grow and become more comfortable with who you are, share your feelings with your wife. It will take some time before you allow yourself to be self-revealing so be patient; growth in relationships comes from such sharing. It is also important to give your spouse quality listening time. Even if you don't agree with her, listening is a tremendous help for a wife when she knows her feelings are heard. Your fear of closeness will diminish as you learn how intimate relationships work to overcome the limitations we all face. Working together with someone you love to solve problems is one of the great joys of life.

Survival Strategies for Wives of Conquistadors

Feeling secure with your husband will require a long period of consistent faithful behavior on his part and some considerable attention to the residual anger in you. While you're unlikely to forget the betrayal, forgive. Forgiveness is for you, a tonic for the anger, and not for him. As forgiveness begins in understanding, listen when he explains his motives, no matter how flawed. Improve your understanding of each other through communication. As the relationship heals, keep the following suggestions in mind.

Don't accept guilt for your "failure" as a wife. Sure, most couples could improve their communication skills but your husband made his decisions as a result of his own problems. An affair is a drastic, destructive attempt to evade a problem and it risks the marriage. Your husband didn't expect to be caught and his flawed reasoning screened the consequences of his actions from him. In some sense he was blind and didn't realize what he was doing. Now, having been caught, he is embarrassed and will act to defend himself by shifting the blame and guilt to others. Don't defend his actions by accepting a part in his misbehavior and don't accept his excuses, either. Your husband needs to mature and accept his mistakes. Despite your anger and pain, if forgiveness is possible then, by all means, forgive him but remember this. You weren't consulted about his affairs and they weren't your fault.

As communication improves, convey all your feelings to him including the hurt, anger, fears, grief over the loss of the man you married, etc. Being open with these feelings are a part of constructing a higher level in your relationship. You have to be able to speak your mind without fear of further rejection from him or fear of counterattacks. "It takes two to tango" is trite, but true. He has to be willing to listen.

You can ease the anxiety on your husband by letting him know you appreciate his gentler side as well. Conquistadors have never been taught to be gentle and they don't associate the strength in gentleness with manhood. It takes time for the Conquistador to learn to be strong when necessary and yet gentle inside the home.

Listening to your husband's insecurities helps. This allows him to open up. He doesn't need reassurance as much as he needs to know he can be open about who he is and still be safe. Don't attack him when he begins to expose himself as the interaction is the beginning of intimacy.

Ask him about the role models from his past. Encourage your husband to develop his own model of masculinity. A masculine male includes a man who can be empathetic, sensitive and fearless about revealing his weaknesses. Tell him this so he knows that you know he isn't being weak.

How Therapy Can Help

The Conquistador profile presents a particular and often difficult challenge in therapy. Typically, they are not aware of any acceptable demonstration of manhood except the immature behaviors into which they are trapped. To even look at themselves as having flaws challenges the very idea they reject. They cannot be flawed. Doesn't their power over women prove their masculinity? When the Conquistador begins to see the flaw in this reasoning, the insight strikes at the very core of who he is. For a Conquistador to continue in therapy is a singular act of courage and a better demonstration of manhood than almost anything else he could do.

Therapy permits the Conquistador to approach his fears under the guidance of person who is not emotionally involved and who is interested in solving the problem, not in assigning blame. This distance between the patient and the therapist encourages self exploration without the embarrassment of intimacy. Then, as self confidence is built and the Conquistador sees his behavior as a limitation to be resolved, he will become willing to test openness and intimacy with others. At this point an understanding wife has the opportunity to be the first person to share real intimacy with him. The experience can be fulfilling to both partners in a marriage.

CHAPTER SIX

Seeking Variety: The Sampler

Variety's the source of joy below,
From whence still fresh revolving pleasures flow,
In books and love, the mind one end pursues,
And only change the expiring flame renews.

– ON A MISCELLANY OF POEMS, BY JOHN GAY,
ENGLISH POET & PLAYWRIGHT (1685-1732)

"Women have an incredible sense of smell," Dale observed nervously at our quickly arranged initial session. "I was shocked and totally caught off guard. I was quietly stepping into the bedroom when my wife, Estelle, confronted me about my mistress' perfume. At 3:00 in the morning, I thought she'd be sleeping."

An intense fifty-two-year-old executive of an oil-equipment leasing firm, Dale was quite shaken. He had phoned his forty-five year old wife, Estelle, earlier in the day saying he was taking a customer out to dinner. He did go out for dinner but with Sandy, his new, pretty, Rubenesque girlfriend from Canada. After dinner, the two lovers went to Sandy's apartment.

"My wife went totally ballistic!" Dale recounted, shaking his head. "First, Estelle pointed out the perfume on me. Then she accused me of running around with whores. There I was, being considerate, trying not to wake Estelle. Nonetheless, she got out of bed, walked up to me and started cussing as she pounded on my chest. 'No wonder you've been taking a damn shower when you come home,' she screamed. 'If you can't keep your schlong in your pants, then maybe I should chop it off.' Then she told me to stay out of her bed!"

Dale called because he felt trapped by his wife's accusations and didn't know what to do. This tall, thin, moderately attractive Sampler admitted having affairs during his entire marriage. However, Dale thought they were harmless as long as Estelle didn't know. Now his twenty-year marriage was awash in open warfare. Dale loved his teenaged daughters and didn't want to lose them nor was he really unhappy with his wife even though their sex life had dwindled somewhat. To fight depression and to invigorate himself, this Sampler opted for affairs.

Because Dale's work limited his contact with women, to increase his opportunities, he had become active in local and state politics. While attending various meetings and fund-raisers, he encountered a variety of women, both employees of politicians and volunteers for their campaigns. He wanted different types of women in order to explore a wide range of experiences in bed and to enjoy the variety of sexual responses. Because Dale desired sexual variety, it didn't matter what the women were like. All shapes and all sizes and all personalities, he just wanted a physical buffet.

The Sampler Personality

A Sampler doesn't simply want women for play like the Playmate, nor for conquest like the Conquistador nor for the orgasm like the Pleasure Seeker. Instead, the Sampler is seeking temporary relief from a very deep underlying depression which

SEEKING VARIETY: THE SAMPLER | 75

haunts him. This depression can spring from his earlier life and, thus, is chronic or it can be a reaction to a more immediate situation in the present. While severe depression is the trigger mechanism, the depression isn't severe enough to incapacitate the Sampler.

For the Sampler, short term affairs involving a diverse

collection of women are an unconscious form of self-treatment. Interactions with a new lover gives him a "lift" but, as the "treatment" wears off, he seeks another "fix" to ward off the low moods. Staying with the same relationship loses its excitement and diversionary quality as routine sets in, opening the pathway back to his despair. Because using women as an antidepressant is a self-centered act, these men are often insensitive to the women who invest their feelings in the relationship.

Initially, the Sampler can be charming and engaging, much like the Playmate. However, he's actually having less fun, he's more easily irritated and he eventually becomes more demanding and pensive. His depressive moods return to drain his energy.

The men who want variety don't need a special type of woman. Young or old, attractive or plain, intelligent or dull, the range is wide; they want variety! Different faces to watch, a range of bodies to feel and see, a variety of shapes, breasts, genitalia, etc., to experience. Single, divorced, widowed or married, the Sampler views all of these women as being eligible. Of course, the more dynamic, attractive women will draw his attention first. However, the Sampler will override his desire for beauty in exchange for the bedding of a different kind of woman. His life motto was summed up in the 1700s by the English poet William Cowper: "Variety is the spice of life!"

On average, the Sampler's affairs tend to be short, from three to six months. Because of the strong pull of his depressive discomfort, it is difficult for a Sampler to have any emotions to invest in a relationship. The focus is on excitement born of variety, not on a meaningful union. The Sampler is looking for a temporary bright moment and doesn't expect great changes in his life as a result of the relationship. His affairs are usually Category One and, occasionally, a weak Category Two.

Samplers equate the brevity of the affair with the protection of their marriages. Even though these men are betraying their wives, the lack of commitment to the other woman is seen as loyalty to a spouse.

In a Sampler marriage sex is infrequent because depressed people tend to withdraw in relationships; pulling back emotionally generates boredom. A Sampler will become bored with his wife, her persona, her body and their relationship. This indifference towards his wife stems primarily from the husband's problems and, instead of dealing with the issues, he'll seek a relationship with a new woman.

When the variety solution the Sampler uses to treat his depression fails, his life only becomes more difficult and no one wins. Everyone: the man, his wife and his mistresses ends up getting hurt. His repetitive pattern creates more and more complications as the mistresses don't like being part of his increasing buffet. Wives, sensing the basic problem, may endure repeated exposures of the Sampler's unfaithfulness.

How the Sampler Relates to His Mistress

The Sampler is more mature than most adulterers. Deceived at first by his apparent stability, his newest mistress may see him as a potential husband, not as a temporary fling. Typically, despite attempts to hide his depression, the Sampler's melancholy will seep out and the mistress will try to be comforting. Because he has a strong conscience which distinguishes him from other unfaithful men, the kindness of his mistress will only stir up guilt and hasten the termination of the affair. Also, when the relationship becomes more familiar and replicates what he has at home, the affair loses its purpose and begins to fade.

For Samplers, depression comes from significant losses incurred at some stage in these men's lives. Through repetitive affairs, the Sampler is attempting to divert his attention from the stress of loss. Thus, the repeated pattern of loss and "reunion" with a new mistress is an attempted form of self-healing while the repeated pain of separation loses some of its sting because it becomes so familiar.

Marrying for Variety

Some exceptional Samplers marry their variety choices. During a preliminary therapy consultation one man revealed his plans to divorce Wife Number 8. Ted refused treatment but he did leave her. Then, a while later, Ted was divorcing Wife Number 9!

Gary, another Sampler with a history of multiple marriages, required an unusual marriage contract. An odd clause limited the legal union to a maximum of five years! Even with an escape clause, Gary sampled various other women while he was married. One wife even caught Gary on the floor of his office with one of his mistresses. That particular episode ended one of his marriages at four years, one year short of the length stated in the contract.

How the Sampler Relates to His Wife

Samplers often just co-exist with their wives. These husbands are simply there but don't demonstrate much love for their spouses. What flame existed between the two of them is usually out once the familiarity begins. Each partner contributes by doing daily household chores and they will have exchanges about the children if there are any. However, for the most part, these individuals are living in two separate worlds under the same roof.

Although the Sampler tries to hide his affairs, he leaves quite a few tracks and clues simply due to the number of women he runs through. Suspicious about his fidelity, his wife will often endure a long period of vacillation between denial and acknowledgment. During this period, she'll have a hard time communicating with her husband while bearing a nagging fear that the truth will be too painful to bear. As their discussions become more and more superficial, the distance between them will increase. Evidence strong enough to penetrate the denial can throw the relationship into ongoing, open combat while, in other marriages, a wife who knows about the affairs may be more pragmatic. While the wife of a Sampler may weigh the benefits of the marriage and decide not to push the matter, her silence does not reflect contentment. She will still be angry and hurt. In some rare occasions, a wife still may be in the dark as some Samplers take elaborate steps to avoid detection. For this woman, discovery will be a severe shock.

Dale

Even during his courtship of his wife, Estelle, Dale was sampling other women to fend off his depression. By repeating the pattern time after time, he reinforced the cycle. To escape detection, Dale maintained an apartment to make liaisons easier when he located available women. At fund-raisers and planning meetings, Dale had a habit of taking a woman's hands in his while cupping them as he discussed a pet community project. This showed his affection and kept the woman present for the whole report while Dale secretly assessed her response to him. He would also sit next to a desired woman at a lunch or dinner gathering. At the end of the meal, there was the little kiss on the woman's cheek and the hug that lasted a little too long.

Dale became an expert in nonverbal communication, using the subtle responses as a red or green light. His success rate was high, in part, because women thought of him as harmless. When hunting, Dale didn't confine himself to any age, size or complexion.

Remember Sandy, the woman who went to dinner with Dale the night his wife Estelle confronted him? Sandy was a "pleasingly plump" 5' 2" but attractive brunette from eastern Canada who was successful in the computer industry. This divorcée with three children was about the same age as Estelle and effused "warmth, receptivity and laughter." Sandy wasn't just looking for sex; she wanted a lover and a close companion. Unfortunately for her, Dale was nice but not Mr. Right. Being an "out of towner," she didn't know Dale's reputation and was left with deep wounds from the affair. However, she survived the break-up and found a good, steady relationship with an emotionally available man.

Dale also described an earlier mistress named June who was a thin, petite blonde volunteer in city government. This widow, who was a few years older than Dale, never considered him as a possible husband. June enjoyed sampling as much as Dale did and they remained friends after she dropped him. So why did the affair end? Dale's depressive moods had kicked in after just a few months and June, having experience, beat him to the punch by calling it off.

What about Dale's early years? As a child, his mother, Victoria, had doted on him. Being an only child with asthma, Dale became entangled in a conflict between being a normal separate person and the desire to please his smothering mother. Then, when he entered adolescence, to Dale's great alarm, his mother began to act seductively toward him. This confused and threatened Dale. He started avoiding his mother by hanging out with friends as much as possible. Dale's father was a skilled worker who was absent from his only son's life. Without guidance from either mother or father, Dale became his own parent. As a teenager, Dale was on his own. From very early in his twenty-year marriage to Estelle, Dale had became so disinterested in having sex with his wife that a month could elapse between lovemaking. As an alternative, he turned his full attention to the sexual variety which was readily available outside the marriage.

After only three years of marriage, Dale was being suffocated by the personal attention his caring spouse, Estelle, was giving him. She was concerned about his mood swings and, while she only wanted to help, her efforts mirrored the activities of Dale's mother and Dale began to see the similarities between Estelle and his mother. In his adolescence "hanging out with the guys" had helped, only now the "guys" were the "other women."

Surprisingly, when the affairs were discovered, their sixteen-year-old daughter, Jackie, sided with Dale, accepting the affairs as understandable. At the time, Jackie was having normal teenage conflicts with her mother and Jackie was worried about her father and his bouts of depression. She told her father that if the other women made him happy, then it was OK with her! A younger daughter, Kate, refused to choose sides and took a neutral stance. It was Dale's wife who delivered the punitive treatment. After she detected Sandy's perfume, Estelle turned up the tension by putting him out.

Keith

A little overweight at age forty two, Keith had good features and an intelligent mind. When in high spirits, he displayed a charming personality and a wonderful sense of humor. At low tide, this man's effervescence would puddle into quiet pools. Despite Keith's moodiness, he'd been married to Beverly for one and a half decades. During most of the marriage Keith had been employed as a front desk manager at one of the larger, upscale hotels in New Orleans. Sophia, a past lover of Keith's who also worked at the hotel, suggested he get help for his "mood swings, irritability and chain-smoking." She warned Keith about "burning out" before attaining the corporate promotions he was pursuing. Even after the affair between them ended, Sophia had remained a good friend to Keith and was able to grin when she noticed his flirtations with other women. To encourage Keith to seek therapy, Sophia told him her own story of effective treatment for bulimia when she was a teenager.

Although bored in his marriage for several years, Keith loved his wife, Beverly, whom he viewed as being attractive but unadventurous. Sex in the marriage had become a low priority for both of them and usually followed a fight. At these times, Keith felt the sex with Beverly was quite good.

The couple had one son together and Beverly was a good mother. He had agreed to lighten her duties by having household help because Beverly worked as a French teacher at a local high school. Keith spoke fondly about their son, Mike, who was showing promise in science in junior high.

Gradually this patient revealed his sexual pursuits. Keith worked in a hunter's paradise. The activities centered in the hotel provided many women as professional groups held meetings or sponsored seminars in the hotel's conference rooms. A travel agency with a high rate of employee turnover was just a block away. An able hunter, Keith's humor amused women so they usually accepted his attentions.

There was one consistent characteristic among his lovers; Keith enjoyed the safety of married women. Still, even with this preference, the characteristic wide assortment, from thin to heavy, petite to buxom, blonde to salt-and-pepper gray, was present.

No matter what profile the mistress carried, Keith always seemed to grow restless soon after the affair began and familiarity was born. As an able hunter, he knew how to play the "chameleon" game with his lovers. Keith's assessed the preferences of a woman and, if she was critical of aggressive men, then he would be passive. If she liked a good talker, then he would chatter.

This man's usual affairs just barely qualified as Category Two, as they were about sex with some mild relationship aspects. On average, the liaisons continued for two to three months. The affair with Sophia had lasted a bit longer than Keith's usual routine; they were lovers for about four months. Sophia was an exception in other ways also. The relationship went deeper and, for once, Keith remained friendly after the affair had ended.

Despite Sophia's variety of lingerie and sexual activities to keep Keith's interest up, he eventually became anxious about exposing his moodier side. After the negative feelings resurfaced, Keith reverted to his pattern. Variety was more important than sex with Sophia and, pointing to the needs of their children, he made the transition from being lovers to becoming "just friends."

Keith's mother had been almost bedridden with poor health and his father had worked long hours and was often depressed. For Keith, the early deprivation of solid parenting was a major issue. To assuage his depression and to distract himself, Keith kept involved with people and chose an occupation which promoted contact with people. While he could hide his depression with humor, this man continually battled the urge to withdraw.

Self-Help for the Sampler

Samplers become bored with sex at home and are attracted to other women. Do you always have a new mistress? Is having a new partner frequently important? Is this sometimes more important than physical beauty?

Do your affairs provide temporary relief from your depression? Are your affairs likely to fall in either Category One or half way into Category Two? Because some relationship is involved in establishing a union, even the limited ones you're creating with female lovers, it is torturous to constantly break relationships. Over time the turmoil only adds to the depression.

Do you blame others for your problems? Blaming your wife, your mother, the "seductive other woman," the pressure of work or what not is a dead-end and inhibits growth.

"What do you really value in life?" The answer to that question will help you uncover the losses which are at the root of your depression. It could be something either in the distant past or from the present. Going from mistress to mistress is one manifestation of loss.

Sure, it's true that having just a single romantic relationship, one with your wife, isn't easy. If monogamous relationships with a wife were easy, then this book wouldn't have been written. One-on-one relationships take thoughtfulness and effort to make them work and thrive. You multiply the challenge with every new woman you take.

Sharing the more explosive material with a trusted friend or family member will be helpful to you or, if this is not practical, you may want to seek therapy. Talking will assist you by putting your entire affair lifestyle into perspective. You'll be protecting your marriage, your children and your sanity. No one can maintain a double life and an integrated whole mind. Ending the affairs will alter your way of relating to your spouse. She may not have known when you were unfaithful but your wife probably felt something was wrong. Now she'll notice a difference in your relationship with her once you decide on commitment. The change in your attitude will give her a sense of security. Be trusting and include her in the process. The exploration and discovery will bring a different and deeper variety to the marriage.

As You Grow: Some Tips for the Sampler in Transition

Your lifestyle may bring health problems: headaches, cardiac symptoms, stomach pain, bowel disturbances, sleeplessness, etc. If so, then have a medical checkup. Meanwhile, expect feelings of loss, sadness, deprivation, anger, conflict and guilt. These emotions have been long buried with the tonic of multiple affairs.

Everyone has their own aloneness as an individual. Since this pattern is entangled with anxiety and depressive feelings for the

Sampler, dependency needs are increased. Yet it's important to become self-sufficient, a point where you can truly love. Mature adults desire love but can survive without requiring it.

Avoid directing any of the surfacing negative feelings in your wife's direction; they're not her fault. You'll need time for quiet reflection. Expect the uplift which will eventually come. The high of having various women will, in time, be replaced with joy which flows from real emotional intimacy and security with that one special person in your life, your wife.

Survival Strategies for Wives of Samplers

If you've been in denial, unwilling to fully acknowledge that your husband might be unfaithful, don't torment yourself. It is human to avoid truth when you know you're risking the marriage, your home and the peace of your children. You may have been avoiding the stress of open confrontation hoping for change in your husband. However, when discussions do start, you may be surprised at how shaken your husband is by how much he hurt you. He may not know!

Alternatively, if you've been clearly aware of what's been going on and have decided against confrontation, then you've probably adjusted by changing the relationship into a superficial one. Most women in this situation back off sexually. While you might take comfort in the satisfaction that can come from with-holding sex, you may be driving your husband more intensely to the other woman and provoking greater eventual anger.

Some wives feel it's too humiliating and painful to open the discussion with their partner. However, with subtle pressures, they may force him to be the one to decide whether to talk it out or leave. Thus, when considering survival strategies, a wife has to decide for herself whether she wants the marriage to work or not. If you do, then explore whether you can support your husband while he works through his problems.

Set aside "talk time" every day. Be actively involved in the communication. Even though he may groan, your husband will actually appreciate the opportunity. Realize that what you may hear could hurt but know that you will be stronger by taking care of your own pain. Showing interest in him, in the marriage and in your own growth is essential for your relationship to evolve to a higher level. If it's obvious that your husband needs more help, then encourage him to seek a professional counselor.

If you're a wife who was in the dark, then hearing the news of a husband's affair is likely to be a painful shock. Betrayal smashes the commitment shared by both partners. It wrecks trust, loyalty and the feeling of being truly loved. You may wonder about your own worthiness and feel rejected. Such feelings, although normal and expected, will create grief and depression. Anger can precede these emotional states or quickly follow them. Often there's a wide range of intense feelings producing psychosomatic symptoms (headaches, abdominal pains, etc.).

At this point, verbal communication will be very important in assisting the reintegration of your thoughts and feelings. This is how healing begins: accepting reality, not hiding or disguising where the marital relationship is at now. In addition, you'll want to avoid generalizing this individual experience to men as a whole. You may be able to trust your husband again or, perhaps, another man in the future. Don't press your husband for details; your hurt and anger will only deepen.

Some wives of Samplers may still love their mates but not want them as husbands any longer. With work and careful thought, you may be able to maintain a friendship of sorts even if you divorce. When children are involved, the relationship has to go on anyway. It's especially wise for parents to avoid hostility by exploring avenues for continued communication. If your husband is difficult, then you may, at least, achieve polite interactions.

In any case, the wife of a Sampler must avoid blaming and

depreciating herself. Men who use variety to deal with their depression would cheat under most circumstances in any marriage. His adultery wasn't personal; he would have done the same to any of his mistresses or to any other woman.

Helping Your Husband Deal with Depression

Because most depression involves a loss (past or present) or a combination of losses over time, help him uncover and identify those issues. Is it about a person, a relationship, his self-image, security or a fantasy regarding achieving one of his goals? Your relationship and willingness to understand can be more important than any antidepressant drug prescribed by a physician.

How Therapy Can Help

Dale

The newness involved with a variety pattern in sex was not the only salve for Dale's depression; he also exhibited a habit of self-aggrandizement, perceiving himself to be desirable to every type of woman. In our sessions Dale enjoyed recalling the various preferences of each woman and the activity they had shared. He liked experiencing a new woman so much that he could forgo an orgasm and did better sexually under these conditions because he wasn't so focused on his own pleasure.

However, with Estelle's confrontation, Dale had become anxious as a possible divorce loomed. He felt the stress of potential social and financial repercussions. Dale was comfortable in the marriage and didn't want to lose his wife, daughters or status.

After Dale sought my help, Estelle cooperated by putting her anger aside to give the marriage a chance. She felt encouraged by her husband's willingness to work through his problems. Still, confused, she vacillated between expressing her anger and acting seductive. Estelle still felt competitive with the other women and was anxious about losing Dale to them. She also feared that his extramarital activity was draining his sex drive. Estelle came to recognize that affairs do not result from problems between the sheets, they begin between the ears.

With therapy, Dale and Estelle moved forward toward a better marriage. As they talked, Dale saw the problems and hurts he had caused and the reasons for his behavior. As he became more open with Estelle, she began to see the adultery as a weakness in him, a weakness which could be repaired, and they began to work together as a team to heal their relationship.

Keith

With time, Keith, the front-desk manager, came to grips with his depression carried into adulthood from childhood. He cried on several occasions, shook with anxiety, cursed in anger, but gradually settled down. As he learned to tolerate emotional pain, his desire for other women began to diminish.

Keith's attachment to his wife, Beverly, revived. He learned to communicate more honestly with her and worried less about her agreeing or disagreeing. His sense of self was developing for the first time. Beverly told him he had changed and felt close to him. Their episodes of "great sex" no longer relied on reconciliations after arguments. Keith felt the "intimacy." Most important, the new intimacy successfully replaced his desire for variety when he experienced the pleasure of healthy marital sex. Love made the difference.

CHAPTER SEVEN

A Need for Independence: The Yankee Doodle

...they are endowed by their Creator
with certain unalienable Rights;
that among these are Life, Liberty,
and the pursuit of Happiness...

– THE DECLARATION OF INDEPENDENCE

"I'm a mess," admitted fifty-five-year-old Blaine, sounding and looking very agitated. "My mistress, I call her 'darling Darlene,' may end our affair. I've been with her for over two years and I'm nuts about her." Just a few weeks earlier twenty-six year old Darlene had announced her desire to marry him. She was asking Blaine to divorce his wife. If not, then Darlene was prepared to "bail out" of the relationship to look for someone else.

Rubbing his forehead, Blaine continued. "Darlene says she can't take it any longer. It kills her when I get out of bed to go home. 'How can you make love to me and then return to Cindy?'

she asked me. The truth is, it's not easy. I love them both."

Blaine had been married for twenty-two years and he and Cindy had four high-achieving teenaged children together. He worked as a stockbroker and did very well. Despite these potentially stabilizing factors in his life, the thought of losing Darlene was very disturbing to Blaine. Curiously, throughout our initial talk, I could see that having the affair helped him feel better about his marriage. Blaine told me directly that being in two relationships fit him better than having just one. In fact Blaine disputed the idea that one man being forever faithful to one woman just wasn't natural.

"I don't want a harem, just my wife and one other woman," Blaine explained. "When I'm having an affair, I'm a better husband and father. Cindy doesn't know about any of this because I'm very careful. I don't want to hurt her."

With four children, it was a tight squeeze to pay all the expenses and Blaine believed he was entitled to the freedom and relief of an exciting, passionate affair. During the session, he voiced no complaints about his wife, Cindy, just the desire for time-outs from the responsibility of marriage.

Meanwhile, Blaine understood the feelings which Darlene was expressing as she had never been married and wanted to have her own family. This man knew he should let his mistress go but didn't know if he could.

"We've always been so loving and sexy with each other," Blaine noted. "I've even told Darlene that I love her, and I do. However, our relationship has started to drive her crazy. Darlene wants a full life of her own and I just don't know what I'd do without her."

Darlene wasn't Blaine's first mistress as he had started having affairs just five or six months after his marriage to Cindy. He described his wife as a good, pretty and intelligent woman. Yet he wasn't cut out to be tied to just one lady for the rest of his life.

"Remember that Cole Porter song, 'Don't Fence Me In'?" Blaine asked me. "That's how I feel about relationships. I want marriage but I'm not going to commit to just one person, not to Cindy, not to Darlene, not to anyone!"

The Yankee Doodle Personality

Yankee Doodles express their liberty and independence through affairs. They equate human freedom with sexual freedom. These men believe affairs are a right to which they are entitled and they tend to see themselves as unrestricted rebels where freedom is defined by breaking some rules. Commitment in marriage is perceived as conventional, conformist behavior by the Yankee Doodle. Freedom from sexual restraint is his natural reward for accepting the routine mundane work activity and the daily grind of family life.

Yankee Doodles tend to be insecure about who they are and use affairs to prove their individuality. In truth, these men lack confidence in their ability to uphold their own self-image and their own identity in a close marital relationship. They equate commitment with dependency and fear being controlled. Thus, liaisons with "other women" support the Yankee Doodle's quest for independent action even while married. The affairs often act as a temporary stabilizing factor in the Yankee Doodle's relationship with his wife.

These men think their affairs are nobody's business in contrast to the Adulteen who has to share his sexual exploits with his buddies. A man seeking affairs for independence will also oppose any moral authority, including the Church, which intrudes into people's bedrooms. Emotional growth is blocked because he has never learned how to tolerate the stresses of a close, committed relationship.

Developing the ability to remain your own person when interacting with another person actually strengthens the personality, the sense of individuality and the independence while making a deep love and intimacy possible. Although many men who have affairs have similar issues, these challenges are more intensely associated with the Yankee Doodle personality.

How the Yankee Doodle Relates to His Mistress

The Yankee Doodle is interested in a one-on-one relationship with his mistress and usually has Category Two affairs. While he becomes involved in intimacy with his mistress, no promise of commitment or exclusiveness is given. The mistress usually knows he's married from the onset of the relationship.

Why does a woman accept intimacy with a man without the trappings which are normally a part of the whole package? Often she enjoys the romance, the sex and the companionship while hoping he will eventually care enough about her to leave his wife. If her hopes draw the mistress into challenging the Yankee Doodle's autonomy and his focus on self-determination, then the affair is in danger. When she tells him what he can or cannot do regarding gifts, telephone calls, sex play, trips, etc., the Yankee Doodle will become defiant and explosive. If she complains and tells him how self-centered he is, then the Yankee Doodle will reply, "No one tells me what I can or cannot do!" This man is very hostile to control by anyone, including his mistress.

During sexual activity with his mistress, the Yankee Doodle tends to force her into doing what he desires. Sex is an intense focus in their relationship and, if the mistress isn't "in the mood" during his time frame, then he will have sex with her anyway convinced that, once they get going, she'll enjoy it. If the woman becomes angry later, then he'll view her protest as insignificant because some evidence of the mistress's pleasure will come to his mind.

To say that their adultery is loaded with difficulties is putting it mildly. In fact there is an element of "attack and counterattack" to their interactions. These couples make passionate love and experience intense differences, as the Yankee Doodle can't compromise because he fears dependency and being influenced by his mistress. This man's sense of independence is closely linked with his view of masculinity.

The Yankee Doodle, as demanding of his own personal freedom as he is, cannot extend his sense of freedom to others. He is inflexible in his attitudes which forces the mistress to either accommodate his demands or to be argumentative and prepared to call the whole thing off. These affairs tend to end abruptly; the final curtain may be dropped at any given moment by either one of them.

How the Yankee Doodle Relates to His Wife

Emotions, like money, can be transferred. If you withdraw from one account to shift to another account, then the balance sheet shows the difference. A wife who has emotional energy transferred from her account to another woman will notice the deduction. She may become depressed, testy and impatient without actually putting her finger on the reason why; she only knows she has less than she had. Some wives of Yankee Doodles view the decrease in passion and romance in the marriage as the normal result of the years spent together when, in a healthy, growing marriage, intimacy and passion increase continually.

In the relationship with his wife, the Yankee Doodle will be dominating and explosive just as he is with his mistresses. He loves her but hates being married to anyone and his wife is seen as a source of restriction. Yankee Doodles make critical, irritable husbands. The discontent with marriage is likely to generate depression. The Yankee Doodle often has sexual performance failure with his wife and, if she doesn't attribute it to aging, then she is likely to blame it on his low moods. Wives of Yankee Doodles try hard to keep the marriage going and to please their husbands but sex usually becomes infrequent and, then, only on his terms.

Psychological Issues of Yankee Doodles

Independence is an important issue in any adult. We begin in childhood by being largely dependent on our parents then, as we mature, there is a move toward more self-reliance and self-determination. In a healthy child-parent relationship, the youngster learns that he'll continue to be loved as he becomes his own person. At the same time, reasonable limits help the child develop self-discipline. Such a balanced approach enables the child to feel secure as the relationships with his mother and father change. However, in most cases this scenario is not what Yankee Doodles experience.

Instead of encouragement, the parents of a Yankee Doodle express displeasure about the growing adventurousness and independence which typifies the teen years. In youth, these men are discouraged from creating a separate, independent identity. This discouragement feeds fear which creates an instability in their self-image. They become confused about their evolving self and threatened when they express their emerging individuality. Such patterns can generate a lifelong struggle regarding closeness and intimacy.

Examples of Yankee Doodles

Blaine

His current mistress, Darlene, had correctly concluded that her relationship with Blaine wasn't going anywhere. Their intimacy was defective because it lacked two important elements: exclusiveness and commitment. While they did nourish each other, the nourishment was for daily subsistence only and didn't promote deep growth. Certainly, it wouldn't support the family Darlene wanted. They had created a relationship in which their romance was based on dishonesty. Darlene had originally become involved with Blaine out of her own insecurities and had found his attentiveness to be comforting and flattering at the time. Meanwhile, he was escaping the confines of his marriage. Now, however, Darlene could no longer deny her feelings of insecurity and guilt. She was losing her self-esteem due to the relationship.

Finding his "companion in freedom" in full revolt threatened Blaine. He wanted to be the dominant, determining person in the affair but, while Blaine was beginning to recognize how deeply discontented Darlene was becoming, he only wanted to continue the status quo based on their attraction for each other. Blaine didn't want to lose either Darlene or his wife, Cindy. Consistent with his Yankee Doodle profile, Blaine didn't think he should have to choose.

Meanwhile Blaine worried about his wife, Cindy. She had a computer business which required occasional travel. As each of her trips neared, Blaine would worry about another man finding Cindy attractive. This jealousy wasn't a measure of his love as much as it was a reflection of Blaine's growing insecurity. A man who won't honor commitment in his own relationship doesn't understand why anyone else would.

This Yankee Doodle had been an only child in a middle-class family and his mother, Beverly, was overly attentive. Blaine described her as very loving but difficult. His father, Jake, was a construction supervisor on large commercial projects. Jake was tough and over-powering and taught Blaine to be tough and ready to fight. As a teenager, Blaine had his share of bruises, his badges of honor, and compliments from Dad. His father had Blaine work for extra money in high school but, rather than letting his son find his own work, Jake had arranged a job for him through his own contacts.

Both of Blaine's parents were smothering and smothered children either become extensions of parental goals or they struggle for liberation. Overly controlling parents exacerbate the Yankee Doodle passions for independence as happened in Blaine's case.

Calvin

Calvin, an athletic thirty-five-year-old sales rep, had worked for a pharmaceutical company since college. Along the way Calvin had also inherited enough money to feel comfortable about finances. As a result, his commitment to work wavered and he took ample time to enjoy his affairs. Calvin's pursuit of other women had started within the first year of his marriage to Wendy and now, ten years later, they had two children.

Over the years Calvin "got along fine" with his parents although they were overindulgent. As a youngster, he won arguments with his mother and father by throwing tantrums and was rarely disciplined. When there was a clash, his mother interceded and gave in to Calvin's wishes while his father only wanted peace and quiet. Without effective standards or discipline, Calvin thought he should have the freedom to enjoy anything he desired. Calvin didn't have any internal conflicts about the affairs; they were his due.

When this Yankee Doodle traveled on business in the midst of an affair, a frequent event, he would take the mistress of the moment with him. When flying, they would go to the airport gate separately and sit in different rows on the plane. Calvin preferred affairs which lasted several months because "dating" someone new was too much work.

At work, a recently promoted supervisor was taking control and more closely overseeing Calvin's work. Suddenly this Yankee Doodle was unable to get as much free time as he desired. His wife, Wendy, suggested talking over the situation at work with a therapist because Calvin was becoming so irritable at home. Wendy wanted her husband to keep the position he had as she felt secure with his employment. She didn't want to move the family for Calvin's work. Their two youngsters were settled in school, they had established social activities, a church and their home was well situated.

In therapy, Calvin was emphatic that marriage was not a

good reason to refrain from "intimacy" with other women. Besides, he told me, it wasn't hurting his marriage and the mistresses were enjoying it too. Wendy occasionally complained about the number of his "business meetings" at night but he felt this discontent could be managed. No one was causing him too much trouble, Calvin said, except that new "gawd damn" supervisor at work.

Calvin's fear of being controlled was evident in his dreams. In one, he was a passenger in a car driven by another man. Calvin didn't know where they were going so he panicked. During another dream, Calvin saw himself in Africa traveling by foot in an area where he feared the presence of quicksand. As Calvin dreamed, he worried about stepping in the wrong place and sinking beneath the surface. He found his dreams puzzling and disturbing.

Self-Help for the Yankee Doodle

Real freedom doesn't distance you from a deep connection to your partner. All freedom includes the freedom from the fear which prevents intimacy with another person. Any healthy relationship requires some interdependency by both people. Hiding in a private castle, safe within the walls, leaves you alone without experiencing a shared love. You are enslaved by your defenses.

Complaints about "the wrong women" being chosen for marriage and past affairs are common rationalizations used by Yankee Doodles. The problem lies within the Yankee Doodle and not within those he blames.

Emotions cannot be controlled within affairs. The Yankee Doodle pattern includes a desire for limited intimacy with the "other woman." Of course, the affair eventually leads to an emotional involvement even when the limits have been made clear to your mistresses. The heart works by itself. Feelings develop anyway, both yours and hers.

Change is inevitable. The affair relationship will either grow more intense or it will fall apart. Either way someone is damaged and, if the affair intensifies, then the risk to yourself, to your wife and to your marriage becomes quite clear.

How well do you know your wife? Do you know the soft spots and sensitive areas of her personality? Is she self-confident? Can she risk honesty with you? Is she happy or irritable and depressed? Does she show trust or is she suspicious of your relationship with her? If she is confused, then your lies may be the cause.

Are you helping your wife grow? If your wife is constantly walking on eggshells with you, if she is guarded, or if she has become withdrawn, then what she's experiencing is regression, not development. On the other hand, if growth is taking place, then your wife's increased self-confidence and self-esteem will be a witness. A wife who is nurtured in a marriage becomes more courageous and expresses her honest feelings and thoughts. Her personality and vitality blossom and the expression of love increases. In which direction is your marriage going?

Try eye-to-eye contact your wife especially during conversation and during sex with her! Poets, philosophers and others through the ages have known the significance and impact of eye contact. The romantic songs about eyes meeting across a crowded room express how frequently courtship begins with a glance. If there is a universal language, then it is the impact of eye-to-eye communication. Indeed, showing your sincerity and love with eye contact is very a strong tonic.

Excessive closeness and togetherness aren't healthy. The freedom to allow each person to withdraw and to even be distant at times is part of the normal human cycle. Healthy individuals, including yourself, need intermittent separation to preserve a separate self within a healthy relationship. Breathing space allows each person room to explore their own growth before coming back with new things to share.

Survival Strategies for Wives of Yankee Doodles

Based upon your total marital experience, you must decide whether or not you want to preserve the relationship with your husband. Don't react quickly to the knowledge of his unfaithfulness but, rather, give your decision substantial thought.

While the human "heart" is always vulnerable in relationships, every crisis is a call for new growth. If your desire is to understand your husband and rebuild the marriage, then recall your adolescence when there were times when you also did secret things in the name of independence. Remember, the Yankee Doodle husband thinks he is confirming his autonomy through affairs outside the marriage. He doesn't see the insult to you.

The Yankee Doodle type affair is seen in men who bring earlier, unhealthy behavior patterns into their marriages. Yankee Doodles have not experienced the normal growth patterns which help youngsters develop their own personality and their own sense of separateness. The exposure of an affair is going to frighten a man who has been aloof because he fears dependency, control and intimacy. As your husband "reshuffles the deck" for more individuality in his character, it will take him a while to accept interdependency. If your husband can talk more openly and honestly, then he will be taking the first step toward a deeper intimacy. You can support growth by keeping the lines of communication open.

The affairs were not aimed against you; they were not personal. The Yankee Doodle perspective would lead a man into affairs no matter who his wife was. Make sure you are continuing your own growth. Don't engulf him and don't be possessive. He will need to separate from you at times just as you will want to be away from him. Nevertheless, be observant. Remember, jealousy is not love. The greater your self-confidence, the more he will want you. Your personal security frees him because he knows you're not glued to him and this mitigates his fear of dependency.

A healthy marriage exists in a growth environment, a Garden of Eden for self-awakening and nurturing. However, there will always be weeds in the garden. Weeds are part of the garden and they are universal. If you move to someone else's garden, then you will find weeds there also. Not pulling the weeds is likely to be part of the pattern between you and your husband so the two of you must learn to deal with things as they come up. Expect the reconstruction of the partnership to be slow. Yet, with time, the two of you can come to terms with your marriage.

As has been stated, affairs don't mean that the man is bad; he simply tried to solve his problem in the wrong way. Yankee Doodles can actually feel frightened by a good wife. They feel guilty if they don't always comply with her wishes. A wife who is a self-confident woman doesn't feel her husband has to agree with everything she does and says. A wife who holds onto her individuality and integrity promotes respect and self-respect lays the foundation for a passionate relationship.

How Therapy Can Help

Blaine

This Yankee Doodle was experiencing very little intimacy with his wife, Cindy, as his main focus was on his mistress, Darlene. While he would have sex with Cindy, she was on the receiving end of a quick and perfunctory performance, what she thought was the typical development of a long-term marriage.

Blaine had never really looked ahead in any of his affairs, the one with Darlene being no different. He cared for, perhaps even loved, Darlene and she had become a source of security and dependency for him. Therefore, her ultimatum about marriage was devastating to him.

During their two years together, Darlene's occasional

inability to handle the affair had shocked Blaine. After a while he stopped seeing her as a duplicate of himself; she had become a separate person. This insight baffled and frightened him. However, until her confrontation, this aspect of their relationship had been, at most, an inconvenience. Most of the time the two had been Siamese twins, and their affair was calm.

Under questioning about previous affairs, Blain recognized the patterns he was repeating. Blaine began to look at himself more seriously, then, as he survived some emotional suffering, he started down the road toward greater self-confidence. From there Blaine's insecurities unraveled and growing intimacy with his wife added clarity and purpose to his self examination. To his surprise, Blaine enjoyed working with his wife, Cindy, to build a deeper understanding.

Calvin

Initially, Calvin didn't readily see how his affairs were impairing the intimacy with his wife, Wendy. Arguing that sex with Wendy was still very good, Calvin defended himself by noting his six month limit on his affairs.

Working with Calvin was a challenge because he did not tolerate authorities well. He didn't understand how the stress in his marriage could be attributed to his affairs. Calvin's wife, Wendy, didn't confront him because she had accepted her life due to her dependency. While Wendy did feel a strain from Calvin's need to control their life, she wasn't secure enough to complain about the lack of intimacy. The other women, being changed every six months, weren't causing obvious conflict either.

Calvin was indifferent toward others as a result of his emotional distancing. He had grown up in an environment which made it easy to remain self-centered. His mother had been overindulgent and Calvin carried an overly independent, undisci-plined lifestyle into adulthood. Yet, without any stable emotionally intimate relationships, happiness evaded him. Using irritability as a guide, Calvin learned to explore his need to isolate most of his feelings. Starting with the work problem he presented, we looked at Calvin's attitude about the new supervisor and then moved on to his wife, marriage, children and friends. In time Calvin experimented by being more open with Wendy and she responded warmly. Their sex life improved markedly and this Yankee Doodle slowly found the intimacy with his wife gave him more joy than anything in any of his affairs had provided. In time, adamant as he was at first, Calvin even developed a friendship with his supervisor.

Most Yankee Doodles have longer affairs than some of the other personalities, such as Playmates or Pleasure Seekers. When their choices come down to independence versus relationship, they'll generally vote to be free. Then, once these men see that truthful, self-revealing communication and self-validation are the basis for both freedom and intimacy, they begin to understand love. Their marriages improve because the husbands are no longer offering the self-centered love of a child. As Yankee Doodles move forward, they become interested in promoting the growth of their wives too. These men begin to recognize their spouses as whole, complex people, not simply someone who is there to satisfy needs. The process takes time and patience but the prospects for a greater prize are better with the Yankee Doodle than they are for the other profiles we are considering.

CHAPTER EIGHT

Addicted to Excitement: The Daredevil

Everything is sweetened by risk.

"Of Death and the Fear of Dying,"

– DREAMTHORP: A BOOK OF ESSAYS WRITTEN IN THE COUNTRY,
BY ALEXANDER SMITH, SCOTTISH WRITER & POET (1830-1867)

Mike, a big hulk of a man, paced nervously. He was heavyset, six-feet tall with a reddish face, a sagging chin and a head of thick, curly gray hair. "A heart attack and bypass surgery last year is the only reason I'm here," the nervous 58-year-old said. "My cardiologist said I have to get off the fast track. Here I am, a guy in his fifties, enjoying life. I have a good family, a pretty wife, a wonderful mistress and now I have to change my lifestyle. It's crazy!"

"I can't see how seeing a shrink is going to help me," Mike stated, as he stopped his pacing and looked in my direction. "I travel a hell of a lot for business and that's not going to change. I don't have problems in my marriage. I like scotch, but I don't go around smashed. The only drugs I take are for my heart. I just like doing things and being with people, especially women! When I travel, I never seem to be able to sit in a hotel room by myself so I find a chick. But now my doctor feels that I have to change my ways."

When Mike first came to see me, he had been married to Blanche for twenty-three years. She was in her late forties and worked as an art teacher at a public high school. They had two children in college. It sounded like an average American family. However, Mike was not an average guy. He was a go-getter with a sharp mind, a quick wit and an easy-to-talk-to manner. Upon entering a new group, he would "work the room." In a short time, everyone knew Mike and responded warmly to him.

Mike had waited tables on weekends in high school in order to buy a motorcycle and then went through a "biker" phase. When riding his motorcycle, Mike loved to weave in and out of traffic and to speed. By the time Mike entered college, he had fractured his wrist once and broken a leg twice. After college he learned to fly and enjoyed doing stunts in a single-engine plane. Luckily, Mike never crashed the plane but the motor did die once. Mike also tried bungee jumping and damaged both his ankles. He hurt when he walked.

The Daredevil Personality

In a way Daredevils are gamblers; they like to take chances. While all people act impulsively at times, the Daredevil can't resist temptation. They are addicted to excitement and are compelled to take risks. While ordinary people learn from impulsive errors, the Daredevil doesn't. Just like the gambler who doesn't intend to lose money, the Daredevil doesn't expect to get caught when in an affair. If his wife does find out about his infidelity, then the Daredevil will be upset enough to promise to change, yet, without the remorse to change.

All of the processes involved in seduction are important elements to the excitement of an affair as Daredevils seek risk-taking to affirm their masculinity and their "magical powers" to succeed in spite of all the obstacles they confront. The affair is a Nintendo game with human players. The man proves his power, skill and control by overcoming his enemies and winning the fair maiden imprisoned in the castle.

Men in this group are able to maintain a stable work and family life and are not antisocial. Having affairs actually works well for Daredevils as an individual. It suits their competitive, sociable, energetic nature and their self-image. Chancy behavior is not just an option for the Daredevil; it is his way of life. Nevertheless, as with all affairs, his behavior comes with a price. The risk taking will impair his marriage and prevent him from achieving deep intimacy and happiness with his wife.

The behavior of the Daredevil may have a medical component as well. Current medical research has identified a chemical reaction which takes place within the brains of people who live dangerously. The chemical reaction stimulates pleasure and the dangerous behaviors common to the Daredevil profile mimic the psychological and chemical responses found in drug addicts, smokers and alcoholics. The chemical euphoria which results from taking risks helps to explain why a man who would be an adulterer anyway chooses to have "risky" affairs instead of some other profile. The medical aspect of this profile, which is present in other risky behaviors, makes the Daredevil affair profile more complicated and, as a consequence, more difficult to address.

How the Daredevil Relates to His Mistress

The Daredevil views sex as an exciting sport. It's physical and passionate but not intimate. He will have a Category One affair as the physical activity in a dangerous situation is the real stimulant. The frequency of his affairs isn't predictable; a Daredevil affair can last up to a year or end in less than a month. When a more exciting situation comes up, the Daredevil will drop the current mistress or try seeing two mistresses at the same time. Keeping a wife and multiple women from finding out about each other only adds to the danger, the excitement, the risk and the thrill.

Career women appreciate the Daredevil's Type A, bouncy personality. He comes across as dynamic, warm, sociable and fun. However, he eyes other women and will be looking even when out with either his mistress or wife. The seductive, impish aspect of a woman's personality is more important to the Daredevil than sex, variety or playing. The mistress will find him responsive as the Daredevil turns up his charm and energy when he is with her.

This type of man likes a mistress to be sexually aggressive; her behavior enhances the Daredevil's excitement. At the same time, the woman's aggressiveness reduces his guilt and a determined mistress creates a "Daredevil team." Nevertheless, there will be strict and narrow limits to any intimacy. The Daredevil does not want his mistress to intrude socially.

The Daredevil seeks risky situations which include his mistresses. If a mistress can travel, then he likes going through airports without being discovered by friends, associates or family members. He'll take chances and the Daredevil and his mistress will have close calls. The danger is part of the affair so, if a mistress changes her sporting attitude, then the Daredevil opts out before a real relationship begins. He'll have no loyalty to her and can be very cold when the affair ends.

How a Daredevil Relates to His Wife

Daredevils try to be good husbands, "providers" and fathers. Not generally overly burdened with developmental problems or immaturity, the Daredevil profile doesn't include the severe psychological damage other profiles have. Typically, the calm security of a stable marriage just loses its "thrill" for the Daredevil.

Like many other unfaithful men, Daredevils lack the knowledge of how to keep the passion in marriage alive and, with the added pressure of being biochemically hooked on excitement, they venture forth to other women.

Daredevil men maintain active sex lives with their wives but the excitement of risk isn't there. They crave new, interesting and possibly dangerous situations as an aphrodisiac. Basically, the marital relationship is convenient and the Daredevil relates to it in a superficial manner.

The Daredevil tends not to be critical of his wife and can actually be somewhat supportive. If his spouse is suspicious of his affairs, then she normally accepts his dalliances because she has much of what she needs in the marriage. She emphasizes the Daredevil's good qualities and accepts the affairs because that is the way her husband is.

A Deeper Look at the Daredevil

As in the Conqueror, the Daredevil's pattern of romance is very aggressive but his thrill comes from the daring adventure rather than from the conquest. Exhibiting grandiosity and self-centeredness, Daredevils gain a sense of control when they survive risky events. They value this aspect of their affairs more than the challenge of seducing a mistress.

The Daredevil's affairs get more complicated when both the man and his mistress are married because the woman has her own triangle. When this happens there's the added danger of discovery by her husband as well as discovery by his own wife. The potential passion of a spouse's fury only heightens the thrill and the subsequent chemical rush.

A mistress who is unstable, a characteristic of one profile of women who are attracted to the Daredevil, sometimes reacts violently when she discovers a second mistress. Daredevils may become newspaper stories about attacks and even murder related to the disenchanted mistress. Getting caught by his wife isn't the only risk a Daredevil accepts.

One element common to the Daredevil profile is a lack of parental support in their childhood during times of stress or frustration. Having learned to create a greater anxiety to overcome a lesser fear as a child, Daredevils repeat this pattern as an adult. The deprivation of adequate parenting is also a signal to the child that he has been abandoned, has been separated from his parents and, therefore, is on his own. Thus, without a safe harbor, the Daredevil learns to distract himself with risky behaviors at an early age and carries the behavior, along with the chemical reinforcements, into adulthood.

Examples of Daredevils

Mike

Mike noticed Ginger at gatherings of a local business networking organization and, later, they both served on the group's member outreach committee. Overhearing a conversation in the moments just before a committee meeting, Mike learned that Ginger was married. Nevertheless, he watched her at group events and saw how sociable she was. Ginger would leave her husband for long intervals and move through the crowd. At these times she seemed to laugh easily and men regularly greeted her with a warm hug and a kiss on the cheek. He observed her interest in talking to men rather than women. When Ginger slipped away, her husband would spend the time in conversation with other businessmen.

Mike marked Ginger for an exciting affair as the idea of sleeping with another man's wife was not new to him. He did this even before he married his wife, Blanche, "because married women don't hang on and cause trouble when they're dumped."

At one networking event, Mike wiggled through the crowd

and briefly talked to Ginger. This Daredevil, following the profile pattern, continued to be subtle and mysterious as he glanced at Ginger's unsuspecting husband. Mike gave Ginger his card during the innocuous conversation telling her that he'd like to discuss some ideas for the committee they were on. When she called, Mike suggested a quick lunch.

Their "quick lunch" at an upscale restaurant in a hotel lasted over two hours. Ginger didn't seem any more eager to leave than Mike did and he thought this was a good sign as they laughed together about the characters they both knew in the group. At one point, Ginger mentioned her desire for more excitement in her life as it had become too routine. Mike considered this to be a not-so-subtle invitation so he told Ginger of his desire to undress her and spend the afternoon with her in a hotel room. She responded, "Why not?" Mike made arrangements for the room and came back for her. They were quiet and subdued in the elevator but went wild once they entered their suite.

Seven months later they were still seeing each other. Neither of them was thinking about divorce as they only wanted the exciting "no strings attached" sex. Mike and Ginger met two or three times a month for a passionate, romantic and friendly interlude. Ginger was adventurous and would try just about anything, including activities Blanche rejected. Confining their lovemaking to afternoons, they avoided raising any suspicions.

Ned

This tall, handsome, sixty-two-year-old Daredevil had gotten his "thirty-something" mistress, April, pregnant. The risk Ned had taken in not using condoms, relying on this PR woman's choice of the diaphragm, was taking a bad turn.

"I wouldn't hurt my wife Sarah for the world! Now what will happen?" Ned worried. "This might get back to Sarah and, if the media finds out, what will happen to my political career?" This was definitely beyond the level of excitement that Ned normally enjoyed. Ned had no intention of divorcing Sarah, a devoted homemaker, nor of losing the relationships with his adult children, now young professionals.

Ned made his position clear to April and, without discussing it with him, she had an abortion. This Daredevil felt relieved with the solution but he had also paid a price. For her part, his mistress never saw him again.

April's decision to terminate her pregnancy reduced Ned's anxiety but, with time, his internal tension rebuilt and the urge for excitement reappeared. Soon Ned decided it would be exciting to pursue Glenda, the attractive wife of one of his best friends. Glenda was also close to his wife and the two couples saw each other socially. For Daredevils, the closer to home, the higher the risk involved and, thus, the higher the excitement. Glenda was a natural choice.

At a party Ned made the mistake of flirting openly with Glenda. Under the influence of alcohol, his wife, Sarah, angrily grabbed a knife from a kitchen drawer to use on Ned later when they got home. Strolling into the kitchen to refill his wine glass, Ned saw Sarah put the knife into her handbag and quickly disarmed her. Later, despite the warning, this Daredevil did begin an affair with Glenda and no one in the group, including Sarah, was any the wiser. The affair lasted several months before his tension returned. Ned promptly dropped Glenda and then initiated an affair with his recently married young secretary, Becky.

Since Ned's business suite was busy during the day, he managed the affair with Becky by hanging around after hours under the pretense of working late. Ned would lock the door to his office and, using the newly re-carpeted floor, he and Becky would have sex.

Throughout his marriage Ned had enjoyed inviting

mistresses to attend networking events where his wife was present. His mistresses enjoyed this, too, as the secret they shared in public excited them as well. The "other women" also liked having Ned see their popularity with other men. Still, because he knew each mistress was "his," Ned felt superior to all of those other men.

Ned wasn't an introspective man. He liked following his impulses without giving things much thought. Because he felt entitled to as much excitement as he could grab, the "excitement addiction" perpetuated itself in the absence of any shame or guilt. Ned was only as discreet as necessary.

In his childhood and adolescence, Ned had been his mother's "little prince". He had one sister, Kit, who was four years older and not the apple of her mother's eye. Without any discipline to teach him boundaries, Ned grew to adulthood without developing a respect for social order nor did Ned see his sister as an equal.

Ned's father, Jack, a skilled laborer at a local shipbuilding company, teased Ned regarding the son's good grades in high school and unsuccessfully encouraged him to go into a trade rather than college. In college Ned joined political organizations to meet young women from other areas of the campus. During these volunteer activities, the glamour of a politician's life started to appeal to him as a celebrity gets more attention from everyone, especially women.

Pursuing women becomes an addiction with a short euphoria requiring repeated fixes to maintain the high. For example, even though Mike and Ginger met over a period of time, once the affair began in earnest, they behaved like drug addicts sharing a needle. There was no concern about the future so they didn't even have to pretend to be in love. Romance was sacrificed for finding relief from depression, isolation, abandonment and anger. Ned could move quickly and easily from April to Glenda to Becky.

Self-Help for the Daredevil

Since you're already sharing the physical accoutrements of life with your wife, why not share yourself with her also? An intimate relationship with the woman you married carries all the thrills, risk and adventure you seek. Opening secret doors in each other far exceeds any excitement you may generate outside the marriage and, happily, the adventure will last for the entire marriage if it comes with commitment and intimacy.

If sex with your mistresses is more exciting than with your wife and, if you feel more sexual excitement is needed with your wife, then tell her! Be open and honest with her and then make it a joint venture of discovery to find out where the blocks are.

With all of that said, Daredevils would do well to get away from the notion that sex is a performance. Such pressure can be inhibiting. Increased intimacy with a wife is so much more important than discussing particular sexual techniques. Many men miss the whole value of a secure, committed relationship; sex with a familiar, trusted partner is the best sex!

The high-energy component of your personality can be very positive when routed into a stable activity. Hobbies, sports and social organizations are among the possible alternatives. Expanding and enjoying friendships with other men will also reinforce your masculine identity as they accept you.

Survival Strategies for Wives of Daredevils

Communicate with your husband. Tell him more about you, the marriage and what you encountered in your original family. Let him listen about the person you really are. Encourage him to share himself in the same way. There may be less sex when these exchanges begin but, as the exploration becomes familiar, better love making will follow. You'll be relating person-to-person, not man to woman on the man's terms. It may still be a man's world in society but there doesn't have to be the same power structure in bed. Equality preserves and enhances the self-esteem of both partners!

When the sexual action does start, don't be thinking of your husband as the father of your children. Just be a man and a woman making love and enjoying all the things men and women like to do together. Daredevils aren't the only people who like excitement. Your husband will get very excited when he sees and feels your pleasure. Enjoy yourself. Enjoy the excitement and he will too!

Being creative will be important. However, if you're going to have shared fantasies for excitement, do it for yourself, too, not just for him. If you think your fantasies will excite him, then share them with him. Ask him for his reactions and then let your husband be responsible for his own excitement. Use the security of loving each other as an anchor and trust each other with private thoughts. The intimacy is the source of adventure and excitement. Explore each other and yield to the thrills you encounter!

How Therapy Can Help

The Daredevil doesn't realize the addiction-like dependency he has on his mistresses. Even so, the hidden dependency lowers the man's self-esteem. As a Daredevil frees himself from his addiction to excitement, his self-image and sense of masculinity will improve.

Be careful of medications. Daredevils who are experiencing boredom and depression express an interest in excitement in order to "feel alive." If these men are toned down with too much medication, then they may respond by seeking an even more extreme excitement! Medications are generally a mask for the underlying cause even when medical problems are diagnosed.

Mike

Mike had undergone bypass surgery and was scared. His doctor had warned him to slow down. Mike was also insecure about being alone and the affairs he was having made him worry about losing his wife. Mike was well motivated to respond to therapy.

As with others who rely on excitement, Mike's focus was on seduction; the risks involved in romancing a particular woman. When sex finally did occur, the act didn't take him very long. Mike was more into foreplay and, through his descriptions of the sexual activity, Mike made it clear that what he wanted done to him was what he wanted done. This man was preoccupied with his own pleasure.

Mike had masturbated frequently as a teen. Once, as a teen, Mike had climbed onto a high, narrow ledge attached to his family's two story house to watch a young aunt who was visiting take a shower. Of course, he masturbated. The dangers of being on the narrow ledge two stories up, of getting caught and of masturbating outdoors were so exciting to him that this episode became one of Mike's favorite memories.

In general, Mike's relationships with his parents were good. His complaints centered mainly on doubts about his masculinity since he had never made a team as an athlete in school while his more athletic older brother did play organized sports and was more favored. Still, Mike was always "a very active kid." Although not a gifted athlete, Mike did receive recognition for his intelligence and his social skills and was popular throughout his school years.

Working with the above information, Mike began to see the connection between his compulsion for excitement and his attraction to married women. To him, bedding another man's wife meant victory over the husband.

Gradually, Mike began to report about passing up opportunities with women as his relationship with his wife improved. She responded to his growth and their communication and intimacy increased. Even his interest in masturbation became part of their sex play. With time, as they settled comfortably into their marriage, Mike's need for affairs was successfully defused. Years later, he was still happily married.

Ned

In the family arena, this Daredevil was more comfortable with his mother. Due to his interest in education, he didn't have much in common with his father, a tradesman. The childhood relationship with his older sister was competitive and the siblings didn't draw any closer during their adult years.

In high school, while Ned didn't pursue any contact sports, he did love the solitude of long distance running and girls were attracted to him. In dating Ned didn't see a girl for long unless there was sex. During his school years, he and his girlfriend of the moment would take chances on getting caught having sex in her parents' home, in parks or in Ned's car.

As an adult, Ned's Daredevil approach with women continued and he would bring his mistresses into close proximity to his wife. Through his affairs, Ned felt aroused, potent and masculine. Meanwhile, he complained of increased difficulty having erections with his wife even when she performed oral sex on him.

Excitement from affairs had helped Ned fight off depression, doubts about his masculinity and residual anger toward his father. He eventually recognized how his competitiveness with his father had built an array of emotions which he kept contained by avoiding intimacy in a real relationship. By turning to and intensifying the relationship with his wife, Ned gained greater peace of mind and more stability. Over time, the marriage improved.

CHAPTER NINE

Anxiety About Aging: The Ponce de Léon

Age...is a matter of feeling, not of years.

– GEORGE WILLIAM CURTIS,
AMERICAN AUTHOR & EDITOR (1824-1892)

Arthur wasn't doing well. "I've been depressed. I'm getting old. Next month is my sixtieth birthday. The company for which I have worked for years has been good to me but it has been sold to a conglomerate recently. The new management wants to cut costs and doesn't need highly paid structural engineers. They're asking me about early retirement and I don't have the slightest idea of what I'd do with my time."

Arthur began to talk about Leah, his wife of thirty-two years. She didn't want him to retire as having a husband "underfoot" would mean a loss of her own freedom. Arthur loved Leah but hadn't had intercourse with her in almost two years. Because he'd been having problems with erections with her for several years, she had given up on sex. Even before that, going back two decades, sex between them had been scarce.

"For almost twenty years, I behaved myself. I was totally committed to my marriage; there were no other women. Then, back in my late forties, I decided that I didn't want to die without having more hot passion in my life. I wasn't excited about my wife, Leah, and sex between us was rare."

He then started noticing women in the coffee shop on the first floor of his office building where workers went on their breaks. "One day at the counter I met Shirley, a vivacious girl in her mid-twenties. Shirley was pretty with long blonde hair and startling blue eyes. Very warm, friendly and funny, she worked in PR. Shirley acted very interested in what I was saying and I liked the attention."

Shirley and Arthur started an affair. She was single and had an apartment not far from their office building. Surprised with his rejuvenated performance while in bed with Shirley, Arthur met her three or four times a month over nine years and would still be seeing her if he could have gotten free on weekends. After too many lonely Saturday nights, Shirley started dating other guys and, eventually, found a steady.

Soon after his breakup with Shirley, Arthur began sleeping with his next lover, Natalie, a twenty-six year old woman he met in the same coffee shop. "I'll tell you, when I'm with these young women, I feel alive," Arthur confided. "I have no thoughts about getting old or dying."

The Ponce de Léon Personality

While women think about their biological clocks running out when they arrive in their late thirties or early forties without having had children, the Ponce de Léon sees his biological clock in much more literal terms. He thinks about the end of his own life, of his own mortality. The end of time for him causes depression and stirs up anxiety. Over the hill means something to him.

When the Ponce de Léon is younger and the cessation of life seems far way, death isn't an operating part of his awareness. Then, in the middle years and beyond, reality sets in. Muscle and joint pains, less endurance, reduced sexual vitality and perhaps a minor diagnosis from his doctor triggers an awareness in the mind of the Ponce de Léon: "I'm getting old." The Ponce de Léon reacts to this phase of life with desperation and begins to search for stimulation which will recapture his youthful vitality and restore a sense of adventure. While some aging men respond by traveling more, by signing up for classes in creative endeavors, by buying sports cars or by taking up a new sport, the Ponce de Léon looks for younger women and sex. By flirting with young women, the Ponce de Léon attempts to restore his virility.

The Ponce de Léon's search is more for a younger woman than for beauty. His doesn't desire a continual change of partners as does the Sampler nor will just any woman do as is the case with the Pleasure Seeker. His usual preference is a woman in her twenties or thirties although an eighteen year old mistress would be quite acceptable. Age is the issue and women in their forties and fifties will be "too old." As the Ponce de Léon will say, they're "just not attracted to older women." Ponce de Léons often have Category Two affairs but the liaison can be a Category One. The relationships tend to last longer because these men are pleased to find a younger woman who is interested in them although they bring baggage into the affair.

Due to their heightened concerns about death and dying, the Ponce de Léon is susceptible to unhappiness, depression and hypochondria on one end of their mood swings and denial or over-activity at the other end. Those who go beyond the reasonable limits of exercise to prove their ability to keep up with the younger men court the very events they dread. Pulled muscles, stress fractures and even heart attacks follow their quest to stay young.

Among the most frequent health complaints for Ponce de Léons is lower back pain and leg pains. However, if an orthopedic specialist mentions degenerative changes in the spine, then the man's anxiety can hit the ceiling. Pessimistically, he imagines that future intercourse will be limited or "may hurt like hell." His worry is more general than just giving up sports. What if he can't have sex!? Jumping from a backache to "castration" is an easy leap for the Ponce de Léon profile.

How the Ponce de Léon Relates to His Mistress

The relationship between the Ponce de Léon has and his mistress will be friendly, passionate and romantic. Often, the mistress would marry him if he would be willing. However, being unavailable for commitment generates frustration in the mistress as does his absence from the mistress' life on weekends and holidays. Yet, ironically, this frustration works to keep the passion going!

Ponce de Léons are kind and appreciative. They buy their mistresses gifts, although not always expensive ones. If the man is wealthy, then he may pay for the woman's apartment and handle other expenses. In one situation known to me, a Ponce de Léon bought his mistress a house and was caught by his wife when, while gathering clothes to take to the dry cleaner, she found a utility bill for the other home in his jacket pocket.

Should the mistress get pregnant, either accidentally or by design, reality carries the fantasy away like helium balloons let loose on a windy Fourth of July. The Ponce de Léon will panic or react in rage. The mistress, not expecting this response, will despair when she discovers this hidden side of him. Whether he is or is not supportive regarding her predicament, he will recognize the trouble the pregnancy could cause with his wife. Sometimes the mistress will opt for an abortion. In other cases, because an element of a relationship exists between them, she'll want to have the baby. As the Ponce de Léon's affairs are typically longer than those discussed in earlier chapters, pregnancy is a definite possibility, especially when the mistress becomes deeply involved and wants to force her lover into a decision. Also, during long-term affairs with young women who are usually very fertile, an atmosphere of familiarity breeds carelessness! It only takes one tiny ambitious sperm swimming to an ovum for the miracle of life to occur. News of any pregnancy changes everything as the man, his wife and the mistress are caught in a drama with no good endings. All are hurt.

How the Ponce de Léon Relates to His Wife

In most situations involving a Ponce de Léon, the man and his wife gradually grow more distant from each other. As the children leave the nest, the responsibilities change and, while this would be an opportunity for most couples to renew their early marriage relationship, these couples usually don't. The woman may engage in more social activities, go back to school or take a job to maintain what she sees as her own freedom. This distance from her husband then turns him to another woman for emotional comfort. The relationship between the Ponce de Léon and his wife often remains friendly while becoming more superficial.

In some rarer cases the wife will be disappointed when an empty nest doesn't result in greater closeness with her husband. Her frustration with their lack of intimacy, which she may have seen as a consequence of child rearing, can cause impatient and angry outbursts followed by renewed concern.

As the Ponce de Léon is disinterested in sex with his wife, he can be relieved if she withdraws physically. His performance problems at home may contribute to the lack of sexual activity with his wife while he's usually having a ball with his young mistress. Wrapped in their own solutions to their own anxieties, the Ponce de Léons tend to be oblivious to their wives' needs for sexual and emotional intimacy. The women who do not know about the affairs usually assume the changes are a part of life and adjust in rather stoic and depressive behaviors.

More on the Ponce de Léon's Issues

The aging process is gradual and marked by subtle changes. The Ponce de Léon is hypersensitive to these developments, reacting most strongly to shifts in sexual function. Like many aging men, he may need more sexual stimulation and take longer to achieve arousal and orgasm but the Ponce de Léon's high level of anxiety about these changes can actually contribute to increased dysfunction. Worrying about performance changes he notices but does not understand, his confusion creates a self-induced magnification of the declining performance.

A depressive reaction to these sexual challenges and to other signs of aging will cause the Ponce de Léon to withdraw and to distance himself from his marriage. Suffering from a blow to his confidence and self-esteem and, believing that his performance will be better with a different woman, it doesn't take long for him to decide that maintaining the marital commitment isn't worth the loss of his masculinity. Then the Ponce de Léon starts his search for a mistress.

In a society which values youth, an aging man is still not excluded from competition for women in their twenties and thirties. Ponce de Léons offer wealth, maturity, stability and adventure to bright and attractive young women who are just as likely to become emotionally involved with him as with a younger man. Thus, men who suffer from depression due to aging are able to attract much younger mistresses.

When a Ponce de Léon starts up with a younger mistress, his world will open up and he will be elated. The mental stimulation stirs up his brain chemicals and he'll experience renewed potency. In these affairs the men rebound from their former heightened anxiety and depression. Their moods will swing high and they'll cling to their mistresses. Jealousy, however, is probable as an aging man competes with younger men for the attention of his younger mistress. She becomes his source of rejuvenation and, as she matures, the family she does not have will trigger her own biological clock. When this happens, the younger mistress will press for a change in status.

A mentally healthy man copes better with aging for several reasons. First, his level of self-confidence is higher and his self-image is more stable. Second, he makes more effort to maintain the romance in his marriage. Third, there's an openness and comfort level with his wife which reduces the amount of sexual dysfunction and gives the couple both the intimacy and tools they need to face aging together. In fact, closeness and intimacy can more than offset the declining sexual prowess and make the mature and healthy marriage relationship even more intense and satisfying than it was in younger years.

Examples of Ponce de Léons

Arthur

Arthur's father, Burt, had a heart attack at forty-two years of age and died of colon cancer in his early sixties. Arthur took care to have healthier habits than his father, who had smoked, who drank heavily and who ate excessively. Arthur's father never reached the senior years and the loss of his father's sunset years troubled Arthur.

During his entire marriage, Arthur had only two lovers. As Arthur expressed it, he wasn't looking for a "stable." If he had someone "nice," then Arthur was satisfied. Meanwhile, he continued to have performance problems at home with his wife, Leah.

This Ponce de Léon took precautions to hide "the business he did elsewhere." Arthur described Leah as a "wonderful woman," nonetheless, if they hadn't had children together, the marriage would have ended long ago. Their two daughters had husbands of their own and, in the year Arthur first sought therapy, one of his daughters gave him his first grandchild.

Arthur was seeing Natalie, a medical lab technician in her late twenties and had been with her for three years. This Ponce de Léon described his mistress as a "slightly overweight brunette with beautiful gray eyes," of French ancestry. Natalie wasn't strikingly pretty but he liked her looks, her pride in her ancestry and, of particular delight to him, her ease in laughter. This young woman was fun and she loved to tease him.

Natalie went to rock concerts frequently. Since Arthur couldn't go with her, she attended these with her own friends and Arthur wondered if she was monogamous. However, unable to command her total attention, Arthur could understand how Natalie would want her own life. As there was a thirty year difference in their ages, Arthur didn't want to risk losing her.

Paul

This 66-year-old management consultant initiated a trial separation from his wife, Lois, after their fortieth wedding anniversary. Lois could best be described as "a bitch" and, while she was beautiful, she could be dangerous. Originally Paul had married Lois because she gave him a great time in bed and was "so good-looking." Now leaving her made him feel "lucky to have escaped alive." During their years together, as Paul learned, Lois was capable of violence and periodically displayed her bad temper with physical outbursts. His wife controlled their social activities and told him what they were going to do and when it would be done. When the couple attended parties, Lois spoke to him in advance about which women to avoid because she didn't like them. Lois expected him to respect her wishes and to show loyalty to her.

While Paul continued to enjoy sex with Lois, life was still passing him by. They were both getting old, but Lois looked older to him. She had more wrinkles in her face and more gray hair than he did. Then, during aerobic classes, Paul found himself picking locations near younger female students in order to admire their trim bodies and high energy. As Lois preferred to do laps at the swim club, he became friendly with several women in the class.

Paul began flirting with these young women and, over time, his behavior became more venturesome. Eventually, Paul even flirted when he was out with his wife which made Lois furious. The flirting aroused him and Lois would benefit when they went to bed. Still, Lois saw his flattering remarks to other women as insults to her. She would overhear him telling them how he envied their husbands which, to Lois, was like saying he wanted to have sex them. Paul protested his innocence.

Finally, a pivotal confrontation over flirting took place at a country club dinner-dance. In its wake, Paul stormed out to his sports car in the parking lot with Lois in hot pursuit. She picked up a loose brick and smashed the car's rear window. Since Paul was drunk, Lois drove them home. The fighting continued all the way there. Later, in the kitchen, Lois swung at Paul with a hammer and hit the back of his head, a blow which resulted in a huge swollen bump. Paul left the next day.

This Ponce de Léon compared his habit of flirting to fishing. Usually, after the initial encounter, Paul would receive a call at the office from a woman. Often the woman would repeat the things he had said at a social event but Paul would rarely remember. Still, just the idea of a younger woman being interested in him fulfilled Paul's best fantasies. Generally, his mistresses were married women and all of them were in their thirties. The liaisons tended to last four to six months and were Category Two affairs.

During his childhood, Arthur's mother, Adelle, demonstrated controlling behavior in reaction to her husband's alcoholism. Periodically, Paul would be sent out to the bars to find his father, Hank, to bring him home while his younger brother and sister learned to stay out of the way. Adelle screamed at Hank as Paul would help his father crawl back into the house. Then Adelle would hide all the liquor in the house.

Even during periods when Hank remained sober, Adelle was always fussing at him, critical of many of Hank's habits and harping on his lack of ability to earn a living. Adelle pushed Hank into changing jobs twice, was bossy about his doing household chores and was clearly the dominant one in the family. Hank died in a car crash in his early fifties and alcohol was suspected as being responsible for the accident.

When Paul first dated Lois, she was a "hot pepper" and very popular. Lois told Paul that she liked the fact that he didn't try to boss her. However, she did control him. Lois had initiated sex. One night, after a month of dating, Paul walked Lois back to her apartment as usual. She said, "Tonight's the night! I'm going to get out of this dress. I'll meet you in bed!" It was over quickly and he proposed to her while they were still naked in each other's arms.

Self-Help for the Ponce de Léon

As your responsibilities at work wind down, this is an opportunity for you to get to know you better. Have you been living as a stranger to yourself? Why not share your anxieties regarding aging with your wife and close friends? After all, as they're having the same experience with the same problem, they are very likely to be both empathetic and supportive. Work together with your wife to understand aging and the purpose of the life cycle.

All living creatures, large and small, animal or vegetable, get older and die. The only choice we have is in how we react to that fact of life. Getting older can impart great wisdom and patience while teaching the joys of the small things in life, the joys we hurried past in our youth.

Survival Strategies for Wives of Ponce de Léons

While it is painful to know or suspect your husband of betrayal, if he has the pattern of anxiety about aging and you love him, then don't make a hasty decision to kick him out. Generally, marriage to a Ponce de Léon has redeeming features and may be worth saving. Such a major change in your life requires time and thoughtfulness. You are less likely to make a rational decision when intense emotions of anger create a "stormy night" in your head and short-circuit reasoning.

Not all Ponce de Léon marriages will survive the infidelity. Regardless of whether the two of you decide to work it out or not, start talking with your husband about aging and about what both of you are feeling. While the affairs might primarily be the result of his problems, this experience may awaken feelings you have also. Read books and articles which reinforce a positive attitude.

Talking about aging is a common ground you both can share and it will build a foundation which may lead to greater closeness. Whenever couples can share their secret, vulnerable emotions and feel secure in revealing their true selves to their life partner, intimacy has its best chance to deepen and grow.

How Therapy Can Help

Arthur

Arthur looked upon his sexual performance in his affairs as proof of an inner vitality. The young women were aphrodisiacs to him. The affairs dispelled his fears of aging and disguised his depression. Sex with a young mistress replaced emotional intimacy with his wife. While his doctor had prescribed an antidepressant for his anxiety, getting him to stop using the medication was not difficult because Arthur feared a heart attack or damage to his mind as a consequence.

Then, off medication and taking a big step toward growth, Arthur discovered his ability to manage his own feelings. Once he saw his dependence upon his affairs and the false emotional lift they provided, Arthur turned to his wife and began to enjoy his marriage as he gained confidence in his ability to manage his emotions himself.

Paul

Paul had carried a lot of baggage from childhood and adolescence into his marriage with Lois. He was attracted to Lois by her acceptance of their sexual activities and by the comfort her dominance as the leader of their relationship provided. While growing up, Paul's mother had been very critical of him, of her husband, of the other siblings and of their friends. Paul's wife continued the role his mother had started. Lois was the strong, confident woman who could take care of him. Paul and Lois did reconcile and their marriage moved on to a deeper intimacy but the journey brought both partners into therapy as the co-dependency attachment needed attention.

For some men like Paul, flirting satisfies a desire for sexual freedom. Within certain parameters, it is a socially accepted compromise within our monogamous culture, yet, getting a positive response enhances a man's image of himself as a sexually active, potent and masculine male. When it goes beyond harmless play and becomes an affair, the man will go back in his mind to the earlier flirtation and blame the woman for the entire experience.

Paul didn't use his provocative flirting just for displays of virility. For the first time he was standing up to Lois who had been hiding her own insecurities by being dominant. She wanted Paul to be strong but he always buckled under. This weakness in Paul disappointed her while Paul was intimidated by her appearance of strength.

In a stalemate for some time, Lois's explosion at the country club flirtation initiated a confrontation which led to a better relationship for both of them. The disappointments they each felt were expressed over many marital therapy sessions. Paul was surprised to discover that his depression generated death wishes toward himself and Lois. His anger bubbled out like steam from the mud pots at Yellowstone. Lois's feeling of inferiority about being a woman and her envy of men were brought to light. Dominating men was one of her defenses. As Paul and Lois faced their vulnerabilities, they learned to be closer and experienced much deeper emotional intimacy in the marriage.

CHAPTER TEN

Searching for a New Spouse: The Groom

Is not marriage an open question,
when it is alleged, from the beginning of the
world, that such as are in the institution wish to
get out, and such as are out, wish to get in?

– THE SKEPTIC, BY RALPH WALDO EMERSON,
AMERICAN ESSAYIST AND POET (1803-1882)

"I've been screwing around through most of my marriage," divulged fifty-three-year-old Nathan, a chunky accountant with handsome features. "I've been married to Rose for twenty-two years and I've been toughing it out for the last twenty. Although my wife is attractive, she's not too bright. Often, I thought about leaving but Rose kept getting pregnant. We have four children now, two teenagers and two students in college."

Nathan married for sex. He was a grad student during the first two years of their relationship and Rose would come over to his apartment for sex. She became pregnant so they eloped.

While Nathan still found Rose attractive, he rarely approached her sexually. Six or seven weeks could go by before anything happened and, when it did, Rose initiated the activity. Other than his physical presence, Nathan was not involved with Rose during their conjugal unions.

Nathan thought it was too late to save the marriage. "After all my screwing around, I'm finally in love with a dynamo of a woman named Hope. She is very bright and has her own business. I want to marry her. I'd give up all of my running around for Hope."

Nathan began to provide some more background on Hope, a vivacious divorcee in her mid-forties with one teenaged son in a boarding school out of town. Divorced for six months, she had caught her husband Bob waiting for an elevator in a hotel lobby with the "other woman." Hope was coming out of a business-women's luncheon when she and her husband spotted each other. Flustered, Bob didn't introduce her to his mistress so Hope spoke for herself. They had a big blowup that night and Bob started confessing things she didn't want to hear. Neither of them wanted to work it out and they divorced.

Nathan had started as Hope's accountant and, after taking care of her taxes for years, Hope began to confide in Nathan about her divorce. Nathan reciprocated by sharing information about the poor state of his own marriage. Nathan and Hope talked at her business, in coffee shops and on the telephone. The affair didn't start, however, until about a year later when Hope was legally separated.

Nathan had never been involved with a client before although some of his lawyer friends actually bragged about their affairs with divorcing women they were representing. This had always surprised Nathan a little when his friends laughed about it. "I was attracted to Hope from the beginning but I never expected to sleep with her," Nathan disclosed.

In the past, Nathan had had many affairs. There wasn't much guilt on the surface because he had always given himself excuses and permission for the affairs. Now Nathan realized that he had been looking for a new spouse all along and his affairs had always involved unattached, available women. Nathan wasn't trying to compete with anyone's boyfriend or husband.

The affairs were described by Nathan as "traditional," explaining that he didn't do anything kinky. For him, an affair was a pursuit of pleasure, like going to a good restaurant. "An affair is nice, clean, pure sex," Nathan said, viewing relationships with women from the Category One perspective. "Men want sex. That's the bottom line, isn't it? Now I'm in a serious relationship and this time it's much more than sex. I really enjoy being with Hope even when we don't have sex. In contrast, I don't enjoy being with my wife, Rose."

Nathan was concerned about "messing up" his children by getting a divorce but time was running out. It was his turn to be happy. "I avoided getting serious with the other women because I wasn't ready for a divorce," Nathan recalled. "And my children were too young. Still, I always thought about what kind of marriage I could have with these women. When I'd get thoughts like that, I would back off a bit. I kept the affairs light and sexy to avoid deeper involvements on both sides but it's tough to do when you want to end your marriage and be free to find someone else."

The Groom Personality

The differentiating theme between the men in this chapter and the others we have seen is the motive of the Groom personality. He's interested in a better long-term future with his mistress and is prepared to divorce his wife. In contrast to the Groom, the other unfaithful husbands are just looking for an erotic picnic to soothe their anxieties, to boost their egos or to balance the reality of their married life. The Groom is unique because he is driven by the fantasy of finding a better marriage. The short-term "flings" are used to sort through what's available. This pattern continues until two events converge: the Groom thinks he's found the right woman and he feels emotionally ready for divorce.

The Groom's affair pattern can be compared to a woman looking for a quality outfit at the right price for a special occasion. She'll take several items off the rack and into the dressing room but only buys one. The Grooms also want a new selection as, in their eyes, their selection in their younger years was wrong. Improved judgment will bring a better fit the next time around.

While other men see their affairs just as an adventure, "having extra sex on the side," Grooms intend to leave their marriages. When these men think the right woman has been discovered, they'll allow themselves to "fall in love" and have a serious affair. If they can't get a divorce or aren't ready yet, then an affair can go on for years until they decide to act. When a Groom is in shopping mode, he's not easily distinguished from other unfaithful husbands with other motivations. However, if the man can be honest with a close friend, the secret quest could be shared.

How the Groom Relates to His Mistress

In the initial phase, the Groom is superficial, the typical Category One affair. He won't open up and reveal his motives to his mistresses. Yet the Groom observes the new woman carefully; he observes her personality, her likes, her dislikes, what problems she has. He's also interested in what she wants. Being on a shopping spree, Grooms present themselves as just nice guys and not as intense, passionate lovers.

As the Groom wants to know the woman and her motivations, he attempts to understand why she is willing to have an affair with him. One Groom learned about a bright, single attorney he was seeing by asking her about her parents. She volunteered, "My father said he'd feel sorry for the man I marry." "Why?" he wondered out loud. She hesitated, but then said, "Well, it's because of the way I spend money." A little later in the talk, he asked, "What would you want in a marriage?" She responded, "A big house, maybe a couple of kids, and maids to take care of everything. I don't have a strong desire for kids, but my parents want grandchildren." That conversation ended a six-week affair the same night. The Groom never called the woman again although she kept inviting him to dinner at her apartment. He was looking for a new spouse and the woman had disqualified herself with her own words.

If a relationship reaches the next phase and the Groom feels he's found the right woman, then he'll open up and start to be vulnerable, letting the affair deepen. He will become emotionally close, intimate and joyous over locating her. The Groom will share the details of his life and the problems they might face. If she really loves him, then his mistress will help him plan their future and will accept the baggage he brings. Their affair will change from a Category One to a Two and perhaps even to a Category Three.

Interestingly, in his search for a new spouse, a Groom is likely to sample divorced women. By selecting a mistress who's been through a marital separation, the Groom can explore feelings he'll soon have to master. Hearing of the complications associated with a divorce may cause him to turn back to reconsidering his marriage or, learning from the mistress' previous experience may enable the Groom to make a successful transition into a new marital relationship.

How the Groom Relates to His Wife

These men are unhappy in their marriages but usually attempt to maintain the status quo while searching. Although Grooms are discreet until they want to provoke a crisis, they can still have episodes of irritability with their wives as they fend off depression and discontent. However, grouchiness may abate after time with a mistress lifts the gloom. The Groom will come home and be more civil, a sign the wife may interpret incorrectly.

Grooms continue to have sex with their spouses but it is more of a routine than an intimate experience. A perceptive, sensitive woman will sense something is missing but if a wife thinks routine sex is just part of marriage and familiarity, she may accept it. On the other hand, if this pattern frustrates her, she will be less interested in sex, a situation the Groom will probably accept because he has another option. Wives who become more distant because they sense an affair is in the works can actually motivate the Groom to look even more actively for a new wife. A wife's efforts to seduce the Groom back into the marriage often don't work as he has been thinking about making a change for years, not months. Many of these men are willing to be kind, friendly and generous in their separation because they simply want out and desire the wife's cooperation. The Groom wants to be seen as a nice guy to diminish any guilt he might have and he doesn't want her to seek revenge, financially or otherwise.

If there are children, then the Groom will tend to be more thoughtful about working through a breakup. Sometimes however, when there aren't any children, the man may act abruptly and disregard his wife's feelings. Still, in most situations, Grooms will show sensitivity toward their wives.

The hurt suffered by a wife who is taken by surprise can be considerable. Wives who plead to keep the marriage can lose self-esteem, becoming very depressed and eventually angry. Later those emotions sometimes diminish and some former wives want to remain friends with the Groom because his friendship is interpreted as acceptance and a form of love. Or she might not recover at all.

A rejected wife's anger can find a wide range of expressions, from controlled verbalization to direct violence. If the marriage relationship has been in gridlock for years but apparently working on the surface, then she will be stunned and confused. In the confusion many wives experience guilt and a sense of failure as they wonder how they contributed to the situation. The confusion can extend beyond the divorce, leaving the wife very vulnerable to either a period of promiscuity or a hasty marriage. Her need to find someone to value her increases her risk of making a bad choice.

More on the Groom's Issues

Grooms become unhappy well before midlife so these are not simple midlife affairs. The embers of discontent have been smoldering for a long time before the flame appears as a search for a more fulfilling relationship. Grooms intend to remarry. This doesn't mean the poor marital relationship is necessarily anyone's fault; some matches are simply a poor fit. In other cases, the couple can be grappling with personal problems they don't know how to resolve.

Bad choices in marriage aren't all that surprising as very few marriages are based on mature, rational judgments. Still, all couples have to work through the baggage each partner brings into the relationship; each person has a past even if it is no more than a childhood history. No one goes through life without some conflict and trauma.

A cautionary note is in order for the Groom, his wife and his prospective new bride. If no one is ever really ready for their first marriage, then what about remarriage? Those who marry and then learn how to make marriage work usually stay married. Those who don't learn how to make a marriage work tend to move on. Second marriages can be much more difficult to manage than first marriages.

Consider this. You don't really fall in love; you grow in love. In mature love your spouse is very important to you and you want to please them, to promote their growth. You're not married for what they can do for you but for what you can do for them. You care about their happiness because you love them! Therefore you nurture your spouse in many ways, not because you have to, but because that's what you want to do. In contrast, the Groom isn't interested in nurturing his wife; he just wants out of the marriage.

Lyndon

At age fifty-eight, this thin, quiet man was considering divorcing his wife Regina. Lyndon had twenty-three years of marriage behind him with two children in high school. An internist had begun to treat him with antidepressants before recommending counseling as well. Lyndon spoke about his depression in a monotone, complaining about the antidepressants because they dried out his mouth and made him nervous.

This Groom worked as an administrator in a large hospital, a job which satisfied him. At work Lyndon had opportunities to meet nurses and other female employees, finding many of them attractive. Lyndon remarked, "My wife, Regina, is very nice and attractive too, but she can annoy me."

Lyndon and Regina had met at the same hospital two and a half decades earlier when she was a nurse and they had married within two years. Later, Regina stopped working to become a mother but was now back at the hospital part-time. "Regina has a lot of friends," Lyndon observed. "People like her. Occasionally, her patients tell me what a kind and caring person Regina is. I agree; she is kind and caring. Sometimes we do have fun together, especially on vacations."

Although Lyndon admitted to some guilt over his affairs, he soothed himself by justifying them. "I'm not having that much sex," he concluded. "There have been only five women in three years." Lyndon described each as "a very comfortable friendship."

"The affairs always start out the same way. We begin to meet regularly in the cafeteria for lunch and, before I realize it, we're bonding. The woman starts to call me at the office and I feel like taking her to bed. I like these ladies and I can easily imagine being married to them."

Since Regina was a good wife and mother, Lyndon was experiencing a great deal of guilt over his situation. However, this man also said he spent a lot of time wishing he were single again. Listing the problems in the marriage, Lyndon began: "Regina talks all the time and doesn't listen to me. She keeps all the television sets on constantly - in every room! This has been going on for years. I turn them off; Regina turns them on. She even likes to fall asleep with the television on which fed many fantasies about picking up each set and throwing them out of the windows. She's a TV nut, an addict! If someone wanted to torture her, then all they'd have to do is lock Regina up somewhere without a TV set."

When Regina came to therapy with Lyndon, she protested that Lyndon wasn't involved enough with her. "He comes home and has nothing to say," she said. The children and sex were what held Lyndon and her together as a couple. Lyndon had become even more detached during the past few years and she wondered if her husband was having an affair. They rarely shared anything anymore except during vacations.

Self-Help for the Groom

One heart-to-heart, face-to-face discussion is never enough. Even if the situation is beyond reconciliation, it is to everyone's advantage to clarify what is happening. The goal should be an honest, open discussion because honest discussions respect both your own sense of self and your spouse's sense of self. To come down hard on your wife only crushes her self-esteem. Nor is crushing a spouse helpful to your own self-image because you will regret the cruelty. Of course, when someone is emotionally injured, the reflex response is to bite back. If you act like an ass, then your spouse will find the labels to pin on your tail.

Survival Strategies for Wives of Grooms

While the prospects of salvaging a marriage with a Groom profile husband are low once he has made a selection, the marriage might be saved with the best chance for recovery occurring before the Groom has settled on a candidate mistress. Your reactions will be important whether your husband confesses his affairs or not. If you've been trying to maintain your bearings in the face of a superficial and distant relationship, then it's time to either initiate an improvement in communications yourself or to be more responsive to efforts by your husband. However, don't expect the problem to be solved with better sex! Men in the search mode are not looking for better sex but a better fit in the marriage. The Groom is actually seeking intimacy.

If discussions about the relationship do start, then be open about your feelings and let him reveal his. Don't put words into your husband's mouth by speculating about his emotions. Listen and allow him to handle his feelings while you handle yours.

Since problems with interaction in a relationship are usually not just one person's fault, it's important not to assign nor to accept blame. Two people can have many problems from their own individual pasts and still interact very well. Take heart in this.

Guard against emotional overreaction by seeking approval elsewhere. Upon learning of their husbands' infidelities, some wives have affairs of their own. Avoid such impulsiveness as the regret and guilt which typically follows "revenge" affairs only complicates the recovery and makes the marriage situation more chaotic. Similarly, clearly assess the situation. Rushing into a divorce will close the door on possibilities for reconciliation at a time when you may not be ready for a final closure. One benefit to facing the marital problems, whether the situation ends in divorce or not, is the new growth which can be produced by resolving a crisis and facing the anger and guilt left in its wake.

How Therapy Can Help

Nathan

In Nathan's case, he had begun to withdraw from his wife, Rose, early in the marriage. Nathan had conducted numerous affairs and this Groom was in love with his mistress, Hope, whom he eventually did marry. Nathan wasn't seeking help for his marriage as his decision had been made; he was struggling with the divorce. Nathan wasn't sure how to deal with his feelings toward the children and Rose.

Therapy gave Nathan the opportunity to ventilate all his pent-up feelings and to learn that he was capable of handling his own guilt, conflict and anxiety. For over two decades, Nathan had lived a life of deception. Admitting the error in choosing Rose as a wife and confronting himself with his life situation had seemed too much to handle. Instead, he had sought relief through affairs. Nathan could pretend that he had another wife, at least for a while. This Groom wanted the other women to soothe him because he couldn't take care of his own feelings.

For Nathan, therapy was important in renewing his self-reliance. Nathan thought his love for his mistress, Hope, would guarantee his sense of being secure. Instead, Nathan learned that it was his own responsibility to take care of the anxiety that comes from the normal challenges of human existence. This is a burden which should not be brought into a marriage by either spouse. The placing of your burdens on your spouse reduces the marriage relationship to a co-dependency arrangement instead of a marriage in which each spouse wants, rather than needs, the other.

By remaining emotionally apart from Rose, Nathan avoided putting this marriage's potential to the test. Meanwhile, this confused man thought his affairs meant he was independent. In reality, Nathan was very co-dependent for his equilibrium on each mistress in a long line of mistresses .

Lyndon

Lyndon had been moving toward divorce without his wife, Regina, being aware of the warning signs, a common blindness in Groom relationships. He was afraid to confront her because he wanted their family life to continue but not in the current arrangement. Both Lyndon and Regina were so intensely unhappy with their status and, yet, very much aware of the potential in their marriage, they were willing to work together toward a solution in order to change their marriage. They didn't want to be where they were and were highly motivated to move to a much better place.

In therapy, Lyndon and Regina were able to slow down and observe their interactions. They saw how their children were being used as insulation to avoid direct communications and self-disclosures. While they were sharing pride in their children, their bonding wasn't one-on-one.

Regina recognized that she kept the TVs on to avoid being with herself as well as with her husband. Lyndon noted that he hadn't been working on the relationship with his wife and had been using his affairs as a way to maintain human contact apart from Regina. The marriage relationship improved and became more intimate as this couple learned to accept and handle uncomfortable feelings. Gradually, Lyndon and Regina replaced their need for the other's approval with self-approval, self-confidence and a better self-image. The walls came down and their life became more exciting and fulfilling.

CHAPTER ELEVEN

Struggling with More Severe Problems: Troubled Men

The greatest happiness is
to know the source of unhappiness.

– A DIARY OF A WRITER, BY FYODOR DOSTOYEVSKY,
RUSSIAN NOVELIST (1821-1881)

"I have a male problem; I go off too fast," Gordon confided. "I heard you were a sex therapist; that's why I'm here." This tall, muscular fifty-five-year-old man worked as a supervisor on an oil rig. He boasted of being tough on the job; his men knew he was "the boss." Yet, that day, Gordon appeared pale and troubled. As he spoke, he resembled a deer caught in the headlights of a car. Gordon's clothes were rumpled and loose, his hair was gray and thinning and his voice was raspy.

He had a sweet wife, Cora, whom he had married twenty years earlier and, together, they had two bright teenaged children. Gordon was in good health as, during regular checkups with his doctors, no physical concerns were found. Gordon enjoyed sex but would become nervous because of his problem with premature ejaculation. Gordon had read about it but, given his good health, had not discussed it with his doctor. "I had this problem with other women before I was married so I know it's not my wife's fault," Gordon acknowledged.

"Cora and I avoided intercourse before marriage," he continued. "We didn't trust condoms and she wasn't on the pill. We are against abortion and definitely didn't want a pregnancy. What we explored instead was oral sex. Cora satisfied me but she didn't want reciprocation."

Before Cora the women Gordon took to bed were all on the pill. In spite of birth control, he felt his premature ejaculation with them was the result of his nervousness about pregnancy. When the pattern continued into his marriage, this reasoning didn't hold and Gordon began to worry about his sexual performance. Now it was taking him much longer to reach erection than it did in his younger years. Gordon was upset with himself and unsatisfied so Cora responded with oral sex once again.

"At one point, my doctor gave me Viagra so I could last longer with intercourse," Gordon reported. "But then I couldn't have an orgasm. Also, I hate taking drugs and am afraid of having a heart attack. I've read about the dangers of Viagra in the newspaper." Despite his sexual issues, Cora remained very supportive of Gordon and told her husband not to worry about their "sex problems."

Almost three years earlier, Gordon had initiated an affair with a woman named Anita. Anita and her husband, Charlie, attended the same church as Gordon and his wife, and the affair started around the time Anita divorced Charlie. Then, after more than two years, Anita confessed to seeing another man for several months. He was divorced, single and available while Gordon was not. Anita wanted to get on with her life.

Gordon's depth of attachment to Cora was not sufficient to resist opportunities with other women. While he knew that Cora was loyal and devoted to him and their family, Gordon didn't feel close to his wife. Finding comfort in his string of mistresses, the affairs made Gordon more relaxed at home and he didn't argue as much with Cora during a "fling.

The Psychological Problems of Troubled Men

Troubled Men who have affairs have other, more severe, clinical problems as well. The anxiety level in Troubled Men is much higher and they have more difficulty relating to others in a consistent behavior. Their internal conflicts produce specific symptoms that, when examined, can be linked with particular mental disorders. The Troubled Man category contains any of the previous nine behavior profiles in association with a separate, but severe, psychological disorder.

The obsessive-compulsive Troubled Man experiences recurrent, intrusive thoughts which compel him to repeat certain behaviors over and over. These inappropriate thoughts and behaviors consume a great deal of time to the point where the obsessive-compulsive's performance on the job and in social interactions may be impaired. These men are programmed into affairs by their own psychological weaknesses. The pleasure of sexual excitement, danger, aggression and approval that they experience in affairs is more than enough to generate a repetitive pattern of pursuit, attachment and detachment. However, while men in this group do have a conscience, it is not sufficiently strong to override the inducements associated with receiving a response and being accepted by other women.

The love and intimacy which might otherwise be available to his wife is blocked by the obsessive-compulsive's preoccupation with his ambivalence about women. For men with the Troubled Man profile, love is eroded by an unusually high level of anxiety. The more threatened these men feel in a relationship, the stronger they are driven toward self-absorption. Their fear leads to a strong need for control and domination of others, which often generates a hostility leading to premature ejaculation and the wish to "get it over with quickly." Curiously, these men seek women as a tonic to combat their fear of approaching the opposite sex, a form of psychological vaccination.

Another Troubled Man profile centers on depression. While all men who have affairs experience some form of depression, the Troubled Man profile suffers a more chronic, severe form of depression. Sometimes this depression can be a by-product of other problems, sometimes this depression can be a primary disorder or sometimes it can be caused by circumstances. For Troubled Men in the depressed category, their depression is usually a lifelong struggle and the origins are likely to be biological.

The severe depression of the Troubled Man causes him to withdraw emotionally and, therefore, his ability to love is hindered. While he might verbalize love, the Troubled Man doesn't feel attachment or commitment. This phenomenon intensifies the man's guilt because he is aware of the love others have for him while he remains detached from them. Tragically, the more love he is shown, the more intense his situation becomes.

Unfortunately, the depressed Troubled Man is unable to use another person's love to nurture his own self-esteem as his ability to be receptive to another person's love is damaged. The anger generated by his imprisonment by life's frustrations is then converted into self-criticism and self-flagellation. Thus, a severely depressed man can be explosive. Men with this degree of depression tend to mitigate their internal pain with alcohol, drugs or women. Alcohol and drugs will weaken their survival instincts which, in turn, makes them vulnerable to disasters including suicide or violent attacks on others.

As we all know from the fabled mid-life crisis, the middle-age phase of life can increase a man's vulnerability to depression with some men becoming depressed because they think their goals were not achieved. Others may be satisfied with their accomplishments and have nothing left for which they want to strive, and women fill this void the depressed man is experiencing.

The borderline personality also belongs in this Troubled Man category. The more severe disturbance of the borderline disorder is characterized by the central emotions of rage and hate which are incorporated into their aggressiveness. In their affairs and in their marriage, this personality may manifest itself as mentally or physically cruel in association with taking sadistic pleasure in humiliating women. (In contrast, the obsessive-compulsive personality expresses his attachment through domination and control, a lesser form of hostility.) Unlike the deeply depressed Troubled Man personality who cannot accept love, the borderline personality Troubled Man profile can receive love but this capability is limited and transient.

The borderline Troubled Man doesn't have the social sensitivity and empathy required for sustaining a consistent relationship and, therefore, is likely to offend others without even realizing it until he is met with rejection, anger and criticism. Men with the borderline personality will have affairs throughout their lives because they don't trust others enough to be emotionally intimate. Being able to turn their emotions on and off quickly, they shut down when too much closeness makes them anxious. They will exit relationships abruptly and completely.

Not being committed in marriage and being difficult to love, the borderline man will feel unhappy and anxious in all of his relationships. His need for control in his life will lead him to handle all the family finances and decisions. His tendency to be too demanding without giving much back leads to divorce in many situations. Those borderline Troubled Man who are able to remain married often do so because of an accepting wife. Meanwhile, he'll have multiple affairs without any specific attachment to any particular woman.

Under stress borderline Troubled Men can become temporarily psychotic. They can develop phobias and hypochondrias or assume compulsive or paranoid behaviors. They may also become involved in sexually deviant activities including sex with minors. A disclosure of these activities tends to shock their community because these borderline personalities are often perceived as normal married family men.

Another class of Troubled Man, the schizophrenic personality, is a severely disturbed individual who tends to be paranoid. Schizophrenics can be very abusive toward their wives, extremely controlling, difficult to please and potentially homicidal or suicidal. Men with schizophrenia will have affairs because they don't feel a commitment to their wives and, therefore, are prone to physical violence.

The schizophrenic's lack of sensitivity to others is obvious to everyone. While he has affairs to satisfy his needs to feel admired and accepted, this man will expect a wife to welcome him back warmly if she is aware of the straying. He may depreciate his wife in the presence of their children without worrying about how this will affect the youngsters while, at the same time, declaring his love for his offspring.

Wives of schizophrenics become very intimidated and frightened by their husbands' outbursts and violent tempers. An unhappy wife may get a divorce from the schizophrenic but she will continue to fear reprisals as her husband will be reluctant to give up his control over her.

Current best science about schizophrenia points to a biological disorder which requires professional treatment. However, as is true of any inclusive description, not all men with this disorder present themselves with these clear-cut patterns. Some are quiet and withdrawn or chronically unhappy. The mental illness of schizophrenia is not just a thought disorder but, rather, a general problem regarding the inability to integrate one's emotional, mental and social patterns.

The final personality disorder in the Troubled Man profile is the psychopath or sociopath. Psychopaths are defined by their impaired conscience so, of course, they don't feel guilty about having an affair. Psychopaths tend to be narcissistic and can be very charming and disarming. These men are dishonest with everyone: their wives, their children, their close friends and their business associates. They feel superior to all people. Skilled at manipulating others, psychopaths often skirt the edges of the law or become involved in actual criminal conduct.

As psychopaths assume that everyone else is just as dishonest as they are, they trust no one. They can't be open and vulnerable in a marital relationship so there's no intimacy. Psychopathic men can go from their wife's bed to another woman's bed with an absence of discomfort. Since betrayal is a "business as usual" situation, they don't have a conflict.

These men are perpetual flirts, always "on the make," and it really doesn't matter if the targeted woman is married or not. Psychopaths don't really love but they are better actors than most. Deception is a practiced skill. If he is good at seduction, then a psychopath will have affairs throughout his life and will readily cheat on a mistress.

Why do psychopathic men marry then? Because they enjoy the conveniences. These men also like the macho image of having a wife and family. When the unfaithfulness of a psychopath is detected by his wife, he is adept at talking his way back into her good graces with promises he has no intention of keeping. Conning a wife is his normal way of maintaining the marital relationship; the intimacy is insincere.

Psychopaths do divorce, often trading in the "older models" for newer, younger ones. These men usually don't stick around for the sake of the children because their tolerance for frustration is low. Within a short time, the new, younger wives will also be betrayed.

Psychopathic men want their pleasures immediately, usually the result of overindulgence by one or both parents. With childhood discipline poor or absent, the psychopath learned early to get away with things. In this profile parents often display greed and dishonesty through their own behavior, thus serving as role models for psychopathy.

In the spectrum of personalities contained in the Troubled Man profile, we see varying degrees of problems. For example, the obsessive-compulsive and depressed men don't actively try to destroy relationships while the more disturbed borderline type does. Some of these personalities can be dangerous to others and can exhibit criminal behavior while others are more benign physically. However, in all cases, the Troubled Man profile is always associated with a bundle of psychological motivations which are more complicated and more severe than the other profiles presented earlier. Essentially, the Troubled Man profile can include any of the preceding profiles combined with a deep psychological problem as well. Any of the basic affair profiles in association with a separate important psychological behavior disorder which would merit treatment all by itself defines the Troubled Man profile and distinguishes it from the other, milder profiles discussed earlier.

Sexual Dysfunction Is Common

The mental illnesses exhibited by Troubled Men often lead to sexual dysfunction because the mind plays such a major role in human sexuality. In addition, when we are sexually aroused, our response is influenced by our attitudes, conflicts, memories, experiences and habits. In short, a Troubled Man's baggage from the past carries over into his sexual performance both in and out of his marriage.

Don't jump to conclusions. Sexual dysfunctions can develop without the underlying serious problems that Troubled Men have and the presence of a sexual dysfunction by itself or even in association with other mild unhealthy behaviors occur frequently and do not necessarily define a Troubled Man profile. Common triggers of sexual dysfunction can be stressful events in the present, a loss of a job being one common example. Frequently, even those with intense conflicts earlier in life can experience improvements when specific issues in the present are addressed. In addition, prescribed sexual techniques often bring relief.

A common problem among Troubled Men is premature ejaculation. While "too soon" may mean different things to different people, in all cases the man isn't able to control his response. Because a medical problem can cause premature ejaculation, if a man notices a sudden shift from his usual control pattern to premature ejaculation, then he should have a medical evaluation to eliminate possible physical causes. Most of the time, however, one or more psychological approaches will be helpful.

In the great majority of cases, premature ejaculation is associated with anxiety and life stresses. As suggested earlier, there may be current conflicts which might need to be explored in therapy. In general men who are comfortable with emotional closeness, love and tenderness are usually able to delay orgasm. Feeling safe and secure with a partner allows the man to prolong the sexual experience and intensify the pleasure. Often it's not an issue of time or technique but one of intimacy and love.

Men with impotence are unable to attain enough rigidity in their penises for sexual penetration or physical satisfaction. This condition is also referred to as erectile dysfunction. Most impotence has biological causes, such as anatomical irregularities, vascular changes, spinal cord disorders, endocrine problems, multiple sclerosis, etc., or it may be a side effect of medication, including antidepressants, diuretics and beta-blockers. However, a certain percentage is associated with anxiety and conflict which may be rooted in the man's developmental experiences which alter his perception of marriage and, therefore, interfere with his ability to relate intimately with a wife. Or, as with other sexual dysfunctions, a current stress, loss of a job, for example, may be a contributing factor.

At the other extreme of the spectrum are men who have ejaculation retardata. These men may have no problem with getting an erection but they can't climax in the vagina. However, they can usually achieve orgasm through masturbation. Retreating to the bathroom alone, some stimulate themselves to orgasm; others masturbate in the woman's presence as part of the couple's sexual activity. Prostatic, hormonal or neurovascular changes, with or without the aging process, may contribute to this problem.

Within the Troubled Man profile a common variant of ejaculation retardata may occur. The man may not be able to ejaculate or reach an orgasm with his wife but he can with a mistress. These men are usually angry with their spouses and the sexual dysfunction is a reflection of those intense emotions. Of course, these men use the ejaculation problem as a justification of their need for another woman.

A man involved in this type of emotional turmoil may even reject a wife's offer to do things to help him reach orgasm. Wives may then begin to blame themselves for his sexual dysfunction and feel inadequate or unattractive. The husbands will be quick to reinforce her self-depreciation.

When a Troubled Man's sexual dysfunction continues into marriage, he is likely to search for another woman just for sex. He isn't looking for a replacement bride or filing for divorce. Instead, the man just hopes that "a new woman may make a difference."

Under these circumstances, a Troubled Man won't be looking for great sex as such but for "normal" function. Meanwhile, as men tend to connect their abilities in bed with their adequacy as a person, prolonged performance problems can affect his self-esteem.

Examples of Troubled Men

Gordon

Gordon noticed Anita ten years prior to the beginning of their affair. Before the affair, Gordon and Anita knew each other well enough for a hug after church services or to engage in a short conversation over the refreshments served to churchgoers. After seven years of friendly encounters, Anita confided in Gordon that she was going through a divorce. She and her husband Jim had grown apart, due, mostly, to Jim's work in the merchant marines which required lengthy trips out of town.

Anita was a very attractive woman, one Gordon had visualized at times when he was trying to excite himself while having sex with his wife, Cora. Gordon liked everything about Anita: the way she dressed, her sense of humor, her wavy light brown hair which reached her shoulders. The sparkle in her eyes aroused Gordon the day he learned of her imminent availability and he was surprised when Anita wasn't severely upset about the pending breakup of her marriage.

One Sunday after receiving the news of Anita's approaching divorce, Gordon attended church alone. When Gordon saw Anita, he discreetly invited her to coffee the next Wednesday evening. As they sipped cappuccinos together a few days later, Anita told Gordon about her difficult decision to leave Jim. She described her husband as a "nice guy" who was good provider. However, Jim was a lousy lover and sex often turned out to be a "wham, bam, thank you ma'am" experience ending with Jim snoring the night away. Also, while Anita suspected that Jim had a "girl in every port," he had always denied any infidelity. Anita expected more attention from Jim and she had overlooked this initially because they had married young and because her family had been poor. Anita was announcing her availability to him!

Suddenly, Gordon was falling in love. He felt passion and excitement. How often does this kind of thing happen? Once in a lifetime, Gordon concluded. Gordon told Anita that he would arrange to take a holiday the next day. The two met in a restaurant attached to an airport motel and soon rushed up to a room. Right after the door closed, they grabbed each other and kissed intensely. Anita dropped to her knees, unzipped Gordon's pants and grabbed his penis. He had an orgasm immediately in her hands. Gordon felt awful but Anita just laughed and attributed it to the initial excitement of being together.

Their affair lasted for almost three years and, during this time, Gordon always reached orgasm very quickly. Nevertheless, Anita always reassured Gordon of her sexual satisfaction. Over time the sex in their relationship turned "cold" as familiarity set in. Their sexual encounters had diminishing moments of passion and Gordon's concern about Anita's satisfaction dissipated. As they were just using each other for their own individual needs, Anita ended the affair when she met an available man.

During this affair, Gordon would use the term "Mother" when he talked to Anita about his wife, Cora. It didn't seem to bother this mistress and Anita would often ask about Cora by saying, "How's Mother?" In therapy Gordon called Cora "Mother" as well and said this was how he referred to his wife most of the time.

Gordon had no real attachment to his actual mother, Madeline. Madeline had been a single parent and Gordon never felt protected by her. Now, although his mother lived alone, he rarely visited her or called her. When he did, it was out of a sense of obligation. Gordon found his mother to be controlling, cool and critical and he carried this backlog of hostility for her into his marriage with Cora.

Gordon had married Cora despite not loving her because he thought she would be a "good wife and mother." His mixed feelings of residual anger and anxiety about closeness kept him distant in the marital relationship and, at those times when there was closeness in their marriage, Gordon would have the urge to find another woman for an affair. The affairs gave him a sense of independence and removed the danger of becoming "too close" with his wife. Responding, Cora learned to keep her distance from Gordon, leading to a stalemate.

Doctors never found any physical causes for Gordon's premature ejaculations and advised him not to worry about it. Since this condition was pushed by extreme anxiety, Gordon tried to get sex with Cora over quickly and was more comfortable with Cora pleasing him orally than with intercourse. Of course, Gordon's fears contributed to his choice of sexual gratification.

Victor

A second example of a Troubled Man is Victor who had an obsessive-compulsive personality. When he sought therapy, Victor and his wife, Harriet, had been married for eight years. This couple didn't want children and were proud of their beautiful dog, Captain Kurt, a pedigreed boxer. Victor was a computer whiz who had a good position with a local corporation. He loved the efficiency of a computer and spent hours seated in front of one every day. (Detail-oriented occupations attract the obsessive-compulsive personality.)

Typical of the obsessive-compulsive personality, Victor had high standards of performance for himself and others and exhibited very little tolerance for the everyday foibles of ordinary people. In contrast, his wife, Harriet, was an extremely friendly and affectionate woman who worked in sales for the same company. Victor enjoyed Harriet's warmth; she admired her husband's "take charge" personality.

Though Victor could be quite stubborn and controlling, Harriet was very tolerant in the early days of their marriage. She would respond by teasing Victor about being so "uptight" when he became critical. In turn, Victor would criticize her for not keeping the house clean and organized with Harriet brushing the comments off with laughter, saying that the weekend would be used for cleaning, and reminding him that she worked also. Victor didn't find the situation funny. He hated disorganization and often lectured Harriet about the efficiency of structure and orderliness.

In bed with Harriet, Victor was serious and determined regarding his sexual performance. As he didn't like wasting time, there wasn't much foreplay nor cuddling afterwards. Subsequent to sex, Victor would tell Harriet that it was time to get some sleep since he always got up early, around 6:00 a.m.

Eventually Harriet began to grow weary of Victor's need to control everything. She started to complain about his rigid over-sight of their spending and aversion to buying her gifts. Harriet remembered his birthday every time but Victor had to be reminded about hers. Arguments worked their way into the rela-tionship with Victor always wanting to have the last word. Winning was important to him. This husband and wife were drifting apart and Harriet found herself wondering if the marriage was worth the effort.

Around this time, Victor began to enjoy the admiration of June, a secretary at the office. He loved June's efficiency and she was impressed with his status. One day June mentioned that her car was being repaired so he offered to give her a lift home. Upon arrival at her apartment, she asked if Victor wanted to step inside for a tour of the place. He agreed and they started their affair passionately.

Within a few months, the relationship cooled down. June didn't feel loved and found Victor acting "cold" at the office. He explained that it was necessary to keep the relationship a secret, especially since his wife worked for the same company. Still, the affair continued. A year later, June decided to relocate to a satellite office of the firm in another city.

Victor requested a consultation because he missed his time with June. While Victor still liked his work, he was becoming aggravated by one of the bosses. Also, his marriage to Harriet was in trouble. He didn't want to lose his job, Harriet or the dog.

This Troubled Man mentioned a much earlier experience with therapy; his parents had taken him to a child psychiatrist when he was ten years old. At the time he was having behavior problems at school and his teachers were complaining. Victor wasn't getting along with other students because he argued continually about the rules of the games they played.

During his childhood, Victor learned to misbehave to get a reaction from his mother, Beverly. Victor recalled enjoying his mother screaming at him. While he had been afraid of her, Victor also enjoyed tormenting her. His father stayed uninvolved, always telling Victor's mother to handle the situation.

Victor's father was often away at work and he would stay out some nights until 2:00 or 3:00 a.m. The son remembered his parents arguing about the late hours his father kept and, in retrospect, Victor thought his father might have been having affairs.

When this Troubled Man decided early in life to declare his independence by rebelling against what was expected of him at home and elsewhere, the tendency became ingrained in his personality. Victor's extreme need for autonomy impaired his commitment to his marriage and he associated his affairs with independence. Harriet was a victim of his hostility and defiance of authority which was born in childhood.

Self-Help for the Troubled Man

Self-help for men with more complex problems is limited. All of the mental illnesses discussed in this chapter, obsessive-compulsive disorder, severe chronic depression, borderline personality, schizophrenia and psychopathy, usually require professional counseling.

For example, the obsessive-compulsive patterns are, in most cases, quite ingrained. Because their controlling behaviors are so much a part of them, it is almost impossible for the obsessive-compulsive person to see it themselves. Then their fear of closeness and engulfment must be addressed and, once again, it's invisible to the individual.

In those cases involving the severely depressed, an outside view is commonly needed to assist the man in giving up his props: alcohol, drugs and women. Depressed men also need to be taught to communicate, to open up honestly with their wives and to allow the healing of their emotional wounds.

However, some specific sexual dysfunctions which are frequently associated with this group of men can often be addressed without outside help. For instance, while a problem like premature ejaculation may have some deep roots, there are simple steps available which a man can apply on his own or in cooperation with his partner. First, recognize that it isn't the length of time spent in actual sex as much as the time spent in the trip which matters. Foreplay and post-coital cuddling are vital expressions of love which do not depend on performance. If worries over performance can be set aside, then attention can then be given to the other components of lovemaking. In particular, energy needs to be devoted to the emotional intimacy between the couple, the most important component of a relationship, not just the mechanics which are minor by comparison. A whole literature on self help with sexual dysfunctions is readily available at your local bookstore or off the internet.

Survival Strategies for Wives of Troubled Men

Regardless of what a Troubled Man's outer symptoms might be, the number one problem for him is usually intimacy. If you're married to a Troubled Man, then you may have settled into a distant and defensive relationship in which the status quo is maintained and seemingly accepted. It will take courage to express dissatisfaction as this requires rocking the boat. Anxiety about your husband's response is likely to surface but the effort must be made if you are not satisfied with the current status of your relationship.

Yes, being open and truthful can precipitate a marital crisis. However, it also creates a great opportunity for personal and marital growth. In contrast, resigning yourself to marital inertia is likely to lead to an unhappy future. Why suffer in silence? If you can develop the determination to open up a dialogue, then there will be rewards to offset the risk.

For some couples, the ensuing crisis marks the beginning of marital growth; for others, it may lead to separation. Some differences may simply be beyond repair. However, for most couples, honesty nurtures the planting of deep emotional intimacy, the kind which really counts. Having such intimacy will enable you to weather future storms in the relationship.

Note that some unfaithful husbands lie about details linked to their affairs to confuse their spouses and to make spouses doubt their observations and feelings. However, dishonesty is a wall which keeps people separate and lonely. Honesty opens the door for intimacy and connection. As a wife, be truthful about your own feelings and encourage the same response from your husband, especially when it may be painful to hear the facts. Often a husband may not be able to confess to having had an affair so, at least, address what has been upsetting you in your marital relationship.

How Therapy Can Help

The majority of deeply troubled men will need professional attention because the personal problems are beyond their understanding. So much of their behavior is so ingrained as to be a part of them and, therefore, invisible to the individual. This doesn't necessarily mean that they'll require long term intensive therapy. The length of the therapy will depend on the patient's motivation, on the skill of the therapist and on the support he has from those around him.

Gordon

Gordon was raised by a single parent, his mother, Madeline. In childhood, while he resented her controlling ways, he had a longing for more of mother's attention. Still, his wishes for closeness with Madeline frightened Gordon. His desire to have a father figure stirred up similarly mixed feelings.

As an adult, Gordon became a clear example of a "control freak." Control became a way to manage his emotions and to reinforce an image of masculinity. This Troubled Man shifted between love and hate, independence and dependence, both wanting love and a relationship and fighting against it. Although Gordon had developed into a very compulsive person, in contrast with most men with severe problems, he did have the capacity to function fairly well.

Gordon responded well in therapy. He saw the connection between what was happening in his life and his childhood history. Eventually, it all became integrated and clear to him. Once he began to understand his hidden motives, he developed tools and skills to manage his emotions and began investigating himself.

This man's relationship with his wife improved as did his sexual performance. With the support of both his wife and psychotherapy, Gordon became more open, he deepened his emotional intimacy with his wife and he no longer needed his affairs.

Victor

In exploring Victor's relationship with his mother, it became obvious that separating from her had been difficult. Leaving the nest is a normal part of the life cycle but Victor had not completed the separation successfully. He was torn between a need for independence and a desire to keep the attachments he had during his childhood. As long as the mother attachment struggles remained buried deep within him, Victor continued to have fears of intimacy. Once uncovered, his childhood history and its connection to his behavior gave Victor an insight to the patterns of his life which led directly to an invigorated growth process. Victor saw how self-centered he had been with his wife and, with time, their relationship improved.

Borderline and schizophrenic patients offer different therapeutic challenges than obsessive-compulsive men or depressed patients. Those with the more disturbed personalities, borderline personalities and schizophrenics, will require an intense and continuous focus on their ongoing relationship with the therapist. The skill of the therapist, as well as his ability to handle being analyzed by his own patient, will be a critical factor in any successful treatment.

Finally, psychopathic types tend to be exceptionally self-centered. A combination of grandiosity and distrust interferes with their capacity for openness and emotional intimacy with anyone, including the therapist. Yet even psychopaths, probably the most difficult profile, can be helped and, as they nudge toward valuing others, they begin to reduce their depreciating and manipulating behaviors.

CHAPTER TWELVE

Summary

Oh wad some power the giftie gie us
To see ourselves as others see us!

– ROBERT BURNS, SCOTTISH POET (1759-1796)

If you're a husband who is having affairs, if you're the wife of an adulterer, if you're the mistress or if you know someone trapped in a destructive cycle of extramarital liaisons, then knowing the type of personality involved will provide guidance if you wish to see the situation change. Whether you want to help yourself or whether you need to make a decision for yourself, having a sketch of the reasons for the infidelity is a useful tool to have in hand. While an affair may look like every other affair to the casual observer, this is not the case and, once the distinguishing characteristics of each of these affairs is understood, it becomes possible to put a given affair into a category. This having been done, it is then possible to identify the weaknesses and injuries which are driving a man to have his affairs. Using this insight, it becomes possible to be a part of a solution whether you are the man having the affair or whether you are the wife, the mistress or a friend. If a solution is only a remote possibility, then this information is also useful as it helps either the wife to end the marriage or the mistress to end the affair. Finally, regardless of the outcome, understanding the dynamics of the situation will promote forgiveness and healing.

The following chart characterizes each affair by its most salient elements. While some affairs share some common elements, every type of affair has its own unique bundle of elements. By separating these affairs by their major characteristics, the type of affair taking place in any given situation can be determined.

10 PATTERNS of MALE INFIDELITY

TRAITS	Adulteen	Playmate	Pleasure	Conquistador	Sampler	Yankee Doodle	Daredevil	Ponce de Leon	Groom	Troubled Men
To be admired	✓	✓				✓				
Pretty mistress	✓									
Dominates	✓			✓	✓	✓				✓
Seeks pleasure	✓	✓	✓	✓	✓					✓
Low frustration tolerance	✓									✓
Instant gratification	✓		✓	✓						
Brief affair	✓	✓		✓	✓					
Mostly sex	✓	✓	✓	✓	✓					✓
Some relationship	✓	✓	✓	✓		✓		✓	✓	✓
Shallow attachment	✓	✓	✓		✓		✓			
Deceptive approach	✓									
Poor lovers	✓						✓			✓
Competitive	✓		✓		✓	✓				
Brags to friends	✓		✓	✓						
Pals with own children	✓									
Non-exclusive	✓	✓		✓						
Depression				✓	✓	✓				✓
Psychosomatic				✓			✓			

Summary Sketch of the Adulteen

Relationships, marital or otherwise, require honesty, dialogue, trust and the ability to promote growth. Living in past fantasies, Adulteens are out of touch with their emotions and cannot trust their feelings. It follows, therefore, that if you can't trust your own feelings, then how can you be in touch with and trust the feelings of others? Openness, meaningful dialogue and intimacy become impossible. There's no real caring, sharing and closeness with others.

The Adulteen is easy to spot as he acts like a teenager by lying and defying his own conscience. Adulteens ride the merry-go-round of teenaged pleasures and superficial relationships. They enjoy the affair game and the rebel against their commitment to their wives. Their daily lives look normal but they have telltale signs of immaturity: tantrums; self-centeredness; lack of loyalty; vacillation between sensitivity and callousness, and periods of extreme dependency interspaced with periods wild independence. Adulteens also exhibit periods of childishness during stretches of maturity. Sexuality is perceived as a game by the Adulteen and he lacks respect for the women in his life, bragging about the details of his sexual pursuits.

The distinguishing characteristics of the Adulteen affair include bragging, a peer relationship with sons and daughters and an unwillingness to discipline children. The Adulteen has the widest range of weaknesses and this makes him easy to confuse with other types. However, the adolescent behavior he demonstrates is an important signal.

Summary Sketch of the Playmate

The Playmate wants a toy. He's looking for a woman with whom to play and he likes lots of toys. Either he will cheat on a mistress as well as his wife, or he will have a series of short affairs. As Playmates see the expectations and responsibilities of marriage as a constriction of their lives, sex with only one woman is a constriction and they will express boredom in the marital relationship.

Playmates want to play outside of the home rather than at home with "momma." While the women they choose to marry are playful initially, when their wives become mothers or become involved in a career, the men then feel that their spouses are not sufficiently available for playful adventures.

These men's affairs are short term as new toys replace familiar toys. When the Playmate becomes bored with or feels too close to any one woman, he goes onto the next. The Playmate will feel secure about entering the new relationship because he lets all of his mistresses know that their relationship isn't serious; it's just play.

The distinguishing characteristic of the Playmate affair includes the most childish behavior of all of the profiles coupled with a resentment of routine. A strong desire for diversion and play clearly marks the playmate in everything he does. The reasons behind the Playmate are less complex than the Adulteen and center on immature play.

Summary Sketch of the Pleasure Seeker

Pleasure Seekers are totally involved in masturbation-linked sexual activity. Sex with a Pleasure Seeker is impersonal and mechanical. Their affairs are conducted merely to experience a variety of ways to reach an orgasm. Sexual activity with various women, including wives, is a disguise of the masturbation pattern continued from earlier in their lives.

As these men are promiscuous in their selection of women and, as just about any woman, body or body part will do, sexuality is separated from a relationship. The Pleasure Seeker's affairs are almost always centered on his own gratification and fall into Category One. There is little or no emotional attachment even to his wife so the marital bond is easily broken. The pattern of affairs tends to continue throughout the man's life.

The distinguishing characteristics of the Pleasure Seeker affair include extreme self-centeredness and an inability to view women as anything but objects which are intended to be used for his own lusts. The Pleasure Seeker has favorite fantasies which he reenacts continually and avoids tiring of his fantasies by changing the partners he uses in his fantasies.

Summary Sketch of the Conquistador

Conquest-oriented men choose "valued" women as targets for sexual seduction. Conquistadors are aggressive, competitive and narcissistic. They go after both single and married women. Because their values in relationships are immature, someone else's woman, a beauty celebrity or anyone perceived as popular or powerful will make attractive challenges for these men.

Initially, the Conquistador envies the targeted woman and he tries to enhance his own self-esteem by first possessing and then depreciating her. This type of man tends to be insecure about his masculinity and may be depressed, irritable and explosive. Controlling women through conquest and domination is his way of countering loneliness and burying his own self-evaluation of his own unworthiness and inadequacy. This fear of revealing his true self then blocks intimacy and commitment.

The distinguishing characteristic of the Conquistador affair is found in the targets of the affair. The women always have some symbol of status such as beauty or social status or wealth. The man, himself, will be a social climber and sensitive to his image. The Conquistador profile is one of the most commonly recognized profiles and is the subject of many myths and stories.

Summary Sketch of the Sampler

The Sampler delights in all types of women. He's bored, responding to an underlying depression which causes him to distance himself in relationships. Instead of confronting his issues, the Sampler engages in short-term affairs. He wants to enjoy a smorgasbord of women without ever coming back to the same "restaurant."

The affairs are brief and the Sampler uses this briefness in his affairs to maintain his denials. As he sees it, he is still faithful to his wife because he doesn't get deeply involved with his mistresses.

The distinguishing characteristics of the Sampler profile are the variety and number of his affairs. He is curious about women and he likes to sample every tidbit on the buffet table. While the Sampler can be confused with a serial cheater who has an endless chain of exceptionally brief liaisons without any attempt to have a relationship of any kind, the Sampler, like all affairs described here, will make some attempt to have some kind of relationship with his mistresses no matter how weak the attempt. Also, the liaisons will last a bit longer than the bed hopping serial cheater.

Summary Sketch of the Yankee Doodle

A Yankee Doodle can be married for years without emotional intimacy as maintaining independence by having an affair is "normal" to these freedom fighters. They want their marriages and are affectionate husbands but they need the support of an affair to feel masculine and confident. These men are afraid of any strong but healthy need for others in their lives. They hide their own problems and consider affairs to be an "unalienable right."

The distinguishing characteristics of the Yankee Doodle profile include a fairly durable if turbulent relationship with his mistress and a tendency to be a better husband while an affair is in progress. The affair validates his freedom and he feels less threatened by the responsibilities of his marriage. This profile is unique in that, while the affair is actually in progress, the man will be more settled, more comfortable and under less day to day stress.

Summary Sketch of the Daredevil

Daredevils are gamblers hooked on the emotional high of risky affairs. These are action oriented men who relish the danger of the journey and the excitement of getting to the rendezvous as the most attractive element of romance. Sex with a woman is less important than the risky process of obtaining her. If the woman is married, then the double triangle, including his wife and her husband, adds to the complexity of the affair and, therefore, to the risk and excitement of the infidelity.

Daredevils are ordinary men in some ways and they usually maintain stable home and work lives but depression and biochemical imbalances are at work as well. The chemical reaction which is triggered by danger enhances the Daredevil's pleasure and it is this "rush" which contributes to his excitement when having an affair.

The distinguishing characteristics of the Daredevil affair include high risk behavior in the affair itself as well as a pattern of high risk behavior in other areas of the man's life. Often the high risk behavior triggers biochemical reactions in the brain when risk is present. The additional pleasure of a biochemical response to risk reinforces the pleasure of the affair. This common coupling of behavior and biochemistry mimics the same coupling of behaviors and biochemistries found in drug addicts and smokers.

Summary Sketch of the Ponce de Léon

The Ponce de Léons try to manipulate the calendar and convert their fantasies of youthfulness, romance and passion into reality. Affairs become a trip back into the exciting world of premarital times. If there wasn't much to those days, then these men will want to have the joys now before it's too late.

A variety of disappointments and concerns regarding work, marriage and health (their own or that of friends) can work to weaken the Ponce de Léon's commitment to marriage and, in particular, declining sexual performance with his spouse. Instead of spending his energy and time working with his wife on these normal consequences of aging, the Ponce de Léon reaches out to other women for a mixture of sex and relationship in either Category One or, more likely, Category Two affairs.

The distinguishing characteristics of the Ponce de Léon affair include the timing of the initial affair, the age difference between the man and his mistresses and the relative stability of his affairs. Generally, while the Ponce de Léon is responding to aging, his affairs are not the product of a mid-life crisis. He fears aging and his own looming demise. When this happens, the first affair not taking place until the man is at least well into his forties, the Ponce de Léon will seek out young women who can be twenty, thirty or even forty years his junior. The Ponce de Léon will be among the most appreciative and caring of the lovers here, the Groom profile being the only other profile which would match the relationship element of the Ponce de Léon yet the nature of the caring differs between these two profiles. The Ponce de Léon will be caring with every mistress while the Groom will allow bonding and a deepening of a relationship with only one of his mistresses, the one he wants to marry.

Summary Sketch of the Groom

Grooms are dissatisfied with their current wives but not with the concept of marriage. They have affairs to sort through the women who are on the market. In doing so, they use sex with mistresses as a way to avoid solving the problems in their marriages. The affairs continue until a strong contender for a new wife has been found. Then he'll begin sharing intimacy with the new woman as a bond forms. Despite their best efforts to keep the emotions sorted out, some Grooms end up in affair relationships that can't go anywhere. In these cases Grooms will want the experience of an intense love which he thinks he has found in a bond with his mistress and, yet, won't want to give up a marriage that involves children. This is complexity at its height and painful for everyone: the man, his wife and the mistress.

The distinguishing characteristics of the Groom affair include the possibility of an exceptionally long affair as this man is looking to take a new wife when the time is right. While he will maintain his emotional distance with his mistresses until he makes a selection, he will begin bonding after the selection has been made. This is the only affair profile which is not based on anger or depression as the Groom sees himself in a marriage with a bad match for a wife. He won't be critical of his wife and he won't be deprecating toward her as he is not angry or hostile toward her. He just thinks they made a mistake in getting married. Given his motives for having affairs, saving a marriage when a Groom profile is involved is the most difficult of all of the profiles and, if he has made the selection before his wife discovers what is happening, the original marriage is almost certainly beyond saving. Nevertheless, after the divorce, it is not unusual for the Groom and his ex-wife to remain friends. While every other profile discussed here involves a man who is hiding from intimacy and closeness, the Groom is actually seeking it

Summary Sketch of the Troubled Man

The Troubled Man profile is a compound profile and always includes psychological disorders which would merit treatment even if affairs were not present. The Troubled Man profile can be any of the previous profiles coupled with a severe psychological disorder.

Sexual dysfunction commonly develops in Troubled Men. Not only do they not relate to their partners well, their confusion about who they are and about their emotions is often expressed in a variety of sexual dysfunctions which are expressed in poor sexual performance. Some of these conditions can be alleviated by the Troubled Man himself, some can be alleviated with the help of a willing partner and some may require professional counseling and treatment.

The distinguishing characteristic of the Troubled man profile is the inclusion of a deep psychosis with the affair behavior. Men in this category have problems so deeply seated that they would require therapy even if the affair behavior wasn't present. The Troubled Man profile includes any of the previous nine profiles in association with any of the five broad mental or biochemical problems noted earlier. The Troubled Man profile also differs from the Daredevil profile which also might have a biochemical association which can be distinguished by the timing of the biochemical triggers. Some Troubled Men suffer from biochemical imbalances which precede and induce destructive behavior while the opposite is true with the Daredevil. His behavior is designed to cause biochemical reactions. Therapy for the Troubled Man can be both lengthy and extensive.

Summary of the Wife

In nearly all cases the wife of the adulterous husband will be blamed for the affairs by the husband who is having the affairs. She will be accused of critical failings which drove her husband to stray. However, in nearly all cases, the wife is not to blame. The husband acted entirely on his own weaknesses and blames his wife to avoid the pain of self examination.

The wife, having been hurt and being confused, will often accept the blame her husband would foist upon her. While accepting at least a portion of the blame is normal under the stress of a newly discovered affair, the acceptance of any blame is generally not justified and can actually delay healing by allowing further denial by the husband. Additionally, by accepting a portion of the blame, the wife also accepts responsibilities for making changes which are not in her power to affect. As the changes must begin in her husband and, as she cannot change her husband against his will, any blame the wife accepts becomes a burden which will frustrate and anger her over time.

If there is any general summary to made about the wives of husbands having affairs then it is this: you didn't do anything to cause the infidelity nor were you a poor wife. You're not to blame. They did it; they're to blame.

Summary of the Mistress

Generally, all mistresses live in denial and false hope. They accept the lies they are told because they have their own hidden motives just as their lovers do. Usually, future marriage is a common goal of most mistresses and it is this one specific goal which the married lover will deny to his mistresses.

Closing Thoughts

I realize that I espouse a minority position when I say that unfaithful men have affairs because of their own personal problems rather than problems arising from a troubled marriage. However, my understanding of infidelity has evolved over more than four decades of work with unfaithful husbands. As I have explained in this book, I saw how the personal issues these men create block the openness and trust needed for emotional intimacy in a marriage.

Flawed and damaged men search blindly for an activity to make themselves feel better and eventually many settle on affairs. Well, aspirin doesn't cure a brain tumor and affairs don't fix mental problems. The treatment just doesn't address the problem. Having more, better and different sexual experiences only avoids getting to the man's core issues.

Fortunately, the turmoil created in a marriage when infidelity is revealed can provide an opportunity for an unfaithful man to gain greater self-awareness, insight and understanding. As a husband increases his self-knowledge and grows emotionally, avenues for reconstructing and revitalizing the marriage will be opened. If the husband and wife use the crisis to learn to work together, then the future of the marriage is likely to bring the kind of closeness which comes from working through a problem with someone you love. Those who have been hurt too badly to trust again and those who do not learn to work together will find their marital differences to be irreconcilable.

For the wife who wants to "work it out," understanding her husband's motives for the unfaithfulness can help as she learns to forgive. This isn't to say that the challenges won't be painful to explore. Yes, love can have its agony, but ecstasy in a marriage can also be found with shared effort and shared dedication. As each person grows, the dynamics of the relationship will be altered.

Also, note that in a healthy relationship, there's a homeostatic balance between needing the other person and being independent. Thus, the degree of closeness and the distance between spouses will vary over time.

Our earth is in orbit. There are certain seasons when it's closer to the sun and other seasons where the earth is more distant. Yet the earth stays in orbit. Our concept of the sun or the earth doesn't change because of our planet's movement. A healthy marriage is similar.

Creating a strong marriage based on mature love requires that each partner have the capacity to tolerate and handle their own vulnerabilities. When both partners are secure, an intimate, close, permanent relationship can exist because both the husband and the wife can tolerate the risk. Self-respect, discipline, integrity, morals and solid values allow trust and commitment to be shared by another person with the same standards.

The mature man doesn't feel a need to be glued to his wife; he respects her separateness as well as her opinions. He doesn't have to control and dominate her to prove his masculinity or his superiority. These traits in the mature man allow him to experience fulfillment in marriage. In contrast, men who link closeness with engulfment fear intimacy because they are afraid of losing themselves. And those who make their wives into parent figures fear being controlled and are unhappy with their own dependency.

In mature love we become willing to forego childish wishes for instant gratification and excitement such as those temporary but corrosive pleasures garnered through an affair. Contrasted with romantic love, the growth of mature love involves a continuous and somewhat slower process. Mature love is an enriching experience which expands our identity and sense of self.

In mature love one can be open and honest about feelings

and thoughts. There's real intimacy so sexuality intensifies with no need for phony role-playing. There's comfort and security in being oneself, in feeling accepted and in accepting your partner.

Ironically, the path of infidelity isn't even the route to the greatest sex! As I have emphasized throughout this book, it's emotional intimacy, not sexual techniques, which is the source of "earth shaking" sexual fulfillment. Mature people who can be emotionally intimate are able to have better sex at any age than the immature person who is too anxious and conflicted.

While commitment always includes the risk of being hurt, the experience of giving and receiving mature love is worth the risk. Loving and being loved are what life is all about! Have faith in relationships, even with all the challenges!

Healing and improving a marriage after the discovery of an affair will take work and dedication. Remember the goal: to build a solid love relationship. The effort can result in big returns. Love is the natural powerhouse of life. Once the powerhouse is rebuilt, the energy will be there, enough energy to last a lifetime.

A Note About AIDS

Sexually transmitted diseases have been around for thousands of years and were reported by ancient cultures as well as in the Bible. However the focus on specific infections shifts with time.

AIDS, the well known and often fatal STD of special concern today, should have changed our behavior in regards to affairs. Did it? In my opinion, no! Perhaps the only things that did change are a greater openness in discussing past sexual partners and increased demands that protection be used.

I do hope that those involved in non-monogamous relationships will take the time to educate themselves about safer sex practices. One good source is *The Complete Guide to Safer Sex*; Ted McIlvenna and Clark Taylor, editors; Barricade Books, publisher.

Suggested Reading

Anand, Margo, and Leandra Hussey. *The Art of Sexual Ecstasy: The Path of Sacred Sexuality for Western Lovers.* J. P. Tarcher, 1991.

Arieti, Silvano, and James A. Arieti. *Love Can Be Found.* New York: Harcourt Brace Jovanovich, 1977.

Blinder, Martin, and Carmen Lynch. *Choosing Lovers: Patterns of Romance, How You Select Partners in Intimacy, the Ways You Connect, and Why You Break Apart.* Macomb, IL: Glenbridge Publishing Ltd., 1989.

Botwin, Carol. *Men Who Can't Be Faithful.* New York: Warner Books, 1988.

Branden, Nathaniel. *The Psychology of Romantic Love.* New York: Bantam Books, 1985.

Calderone, Mary S., and Eric W. Johnson. *The Family Book about Sexuality.* New York: Harper & Row, 1981.

Chia, Mantak, ed., Maneewan Chia, Douglas Abrams, and Rachel Abrams. *The Multi-Orgasmic Couple: Sexual Secrets Every Couple Should Know.* San Francisco: Harper, 2000.

Cook, Mark, and Robert McHenry. *Sexual Attraction.* Oxford: Pergamon Press, 1978.

Edell, Ronnie. *How to Save Your Marriage from an Affair.* New York: Kensington Pub. Co., 1995.

Flowers, Gennifer. *Sleeping with the President: My Intimate Years with Bill Clinton.* Anonymous Press, 1998.

Gathorne-Hardy, Jonathan. *Love, Sex, Marriage, and Divorce.* New York: Summit Books, 1981.

Gaylin, Willard. *Rediscovering Love.* New York: Viking Penguin, Inc., 1986.

Gaylin, Willard, and Ethel Person, eds. *Passionate Attachments.* New York: The Free Press, 1987.

Gottman, John M., and Nan Silver. *The Seven Principles for Making Marriage Work.* New York: Three Rivers Press, 1999.

Greenspan, Stanley I., and George H. Pollack, eds. *The Course of Life, 4.* Madison, CT: International University Press, Inc., 1991.

Greenwald, Jerry. Creative Intimacy: *How to Break the Patterns that Poison Your Relationships.* New York: Simon & Schuster, 1975.

Harley, Willard F., Jr. *His Needs, Her Needs: Building an Affair-Proof Marriage.* Fleming H. Revell Co., 2001.

Janus, Samuel S., and Cynthia L. Janus (Contributor). *The Janus Report on Sexual Behavior.* New York: John Wiley & Sons, Inc., 1994.

Kaplan, Helen S. *How to Overcome Premature Ejaculation.* Brunner/Mazel, Inc., 1989.

_____. *The New Sex Therapy: Active Treatment for Sexual Dysfunction.* New York: Brunner/Mazel, Inc., 1974.

Kaufman, Sharon R. *The Ageless Self: Sources of Meaning in Late Life.* Madison, WI: The University of Wisconsin Press, 1994.

Kelly, Virginia Clinton, and James Morgan. *Leading with My Heart: My Life.* New York: Simon & Schuster, 1994.

Kernberg, Otto F. *Aggression in Personality Disorders and Perversions.* New Haven, CT: Yale University Press, 1993.

Kiley, Dan. *The Peter Pan Syndrome: Men Who Have Never Grown Up.* New York: Avon Books, 1983.

Kuriansky, Judy. *Generation Sex: America's Hottest Sex Therapist Answers the Hottest Questions about Sex.* New York: Harper Collins, 1997.

Lasch, Christopher. *The Culture of Narcissism: American Life in an Age of Diminishing Expectations.* New York: W. W. Norton & Co., Inc., 1991.

Lawson, Annette. *Adultery: An Analysis of Love and Betrayal.* New York: Basic Books, Inc., 1988.

Leary, Robin. "Masturbation and Orgasm." [Interview with Dr. Irwin M. Marcus] *Harper's Bazaar*, April 1980, pp. 153-201.

Lieberman, Carole, and Lisa C. Cool. *Bad Boys: Why We Love Them, How to Live with Them, and When to Leave Them.* New York: Signet Books, 1998.

Linquist, Luann. *Secret Lovers: Affairs Happen, How to Cope.* Jossey-Bass, 1999.

Lusterman, Don-David. *Infidelity: A Survival Guide.* New York: MJF Books, 1998.

Marcus, Irwin M., M.D., Niles Newton, Ph.D., Paul Gyorgy, M.D., and Thaddeus L. Montgomery, M.D. *The Family Book of Child Care.* New York: Harper & Brothers, Inc., 1957.

_____. "Transition from School to Work." In G. Caplan, ed., *The American Handbook of Psychiatry, 2.* New York: Basic Books Inc., 1969.

_____. *Currents in Psychoanalysis.* Madison, CT: International University Press, Inc., 1971.

_____. "The Marriage Separation Pendulum." In Dr. Irwin M. Marcus, ed., *Currents in Psychoanalysis.* Madison, CT: International University Press, Inc., 1971.

_____, and John J. Francis, eds., *Masturbation: From Infancy to Senescence.* Madison, CT: International University Press, Inc., 1975.

_____. "Countertransference and the Psychoanalytic Process in Children and Adolescents." In *The Psychoanalytic Study of the Child,* 35. New Haven, CT: Yale University Press, 1980.

_____. "Harmony vs. Discord in Marriage: A View of Physicians' Marriages." *Journal of Louisiana State Medical Society,* 132 (11), November 1980, pp. 173-178.

_____. "The Need for Flexibility in Marriage." *Human Sexuality,* September 1983, pp. 120-128.

_____. "Masturbation in Adult Life." In B. Wolman, ed., *International Encyclopedia of Psychiatry, Psychology, Psychoanalysis, and Neurology,* 1. New York: Aesculapius Publishers, 1983.

_____. "Emotional and Psychological Implications of *Trauma in Children.*" In R. Marcus, ed., Trauma in Children. Rockville, MD: Aspen Publishers, 1986.

_____. "The Influence of Family Dynamics on Adolescent Learning Disorders." In S. Greenspan & G. Pollack, eds., *The Course of Life: Vol. 4. Adolescence.* Madison, CT: International University Press, Inc., 1991.

Marcus, Randall E. *Orthopaedics.* Los Angeles: Practice Management Info. Inc., 1991.

Margulis, Lynn, and Dorion Sagan. *Mystery Dance: On the Evolution of Human Sexuality.* New York: Summit Books, 1991.

Mascetti, Manuela Dunn. *The Kama Sutra Box: The Rules of Love and Erotic Practice with Each Other.* Harmony Books, 2001.

May, Robert. *Sex and Fantasy: Patterns of Male and Female Development.* New York: W. W. Norton & Co., 1980.

McCary, James. *Human Sexuality.* New York: D. Van Nostrand Co., 1973.

McGann, Eileen. "Let he who is without sin ." *Time.* September 1996.

McGraw, Phillip C. *Relationship Rescue: A Seven-Step Strategy for Reconnecting with Your Partner.* New York: Hyperion, 2000.

McIlvenna, Ted, and Clark Taylor, eds. *The Complete Guide to Safer Sex.* Barricade Books, 1999.

Nowinski, Joseph. *A Lifelong Love Affair: Keeping Sexual Desire Alive in Your Relationship.* New York: W. W. Norton & Co., Inc., 1989.

Pittman, Frank. *Private Lies: Infidelity and the Betrayal of Intimacy.* New York: W. W. Norton & Co., 1990.

_____. *Man Enough: Fathers, Sons, and the Search for Masculinity.* New York: A Perigee Book, 1993.

Ramey, James W. *Intimate Friendships.* Englewood Cliffs, N.J.: Prentice- Hall, Inc., 1976.

Reinisch, June M. *The Kinsey Institute New Report on Sex: What You Must Know to Be Sexually Literate.* New York: St. Martin's Press, 1991.

Rothstein, Arnold. *The Narcissistic Pursuit of Perfection.* Psychosocial Press, 1999.

Sager, Clifford J., and Bernice Hunt. *Intimate Partners: Hidden Patterns in Love Relationships.* New York: McGraw-Hill Book Co., 1981.

Sarnoff, Suzanne, and Irving Sarnoff. *Sexual Excitement and Sexual Peace.* New York: M. Evans & Co., 1981.

Schmarch, David. *Passionate Marriage: Love, Sex, and Intimacy in Emotionally Committed Relationships.* New York: W. W. Norton & Co., 1998.

Solomon, Marion F. *Narcissism and Intimacy: Love and Marriage in an Age of Confusion.* New York: W. W. Norton & Co., Inc., 1989.

Spring, Janis A. and Michael Spring. *After the Affair: Healing the Pain and Rebuilding Trust When a Partner Has Been Unfaithful.* New York: Harper Collins Pub. Inc., 1996.

Staheli, Lana. *Triangles: Understanding, Preventing and Surviving an Affair.* New York. Harper Collins Pub. Inc., 1995.

Wallerstein, Judith S., Julia M. Lewis, Sandra Blakeslee, and Jul Lewis. *The Unexpected Legacy of Divorce.* Hyperion, 2000.

Weil, Bonnie E., and Ruth Winter. *Adultery, The Forgivable Sin.* Norwalk, CT: Hastings House, 1994.

Zehner, H. "What Makes a Marriage Work?" [Interview with Irwin M. Marcus.] *Cosmopolitan,* June 1982, pp. 220-223.

About the Author

Dr. Irwin Marcus serves as Emeritus Clinical Professor at LSU and is a Distinguished Life Fellow of the American Psychiatric Association. He has taught at Columbia University, Tulane University College of Medicine, and Louisiana State University Medical School, and he has lectured around the world as a visiting professor.

Dr. Marcus is a founder and former president of the New Orleans Psychoanalytic Institute and has served on the Board of Professional Standards, as well as the Executive Council of the American Psychoanalytic Association. He was the Founding Chairman of Tulane University Medical School (Family Study Unit) Child Adolescent Program and, in 1996, a lectureship was established in his name by the Psychoanalytic Institute.